The Beginner's Guide to

STAMP
COLLECTING

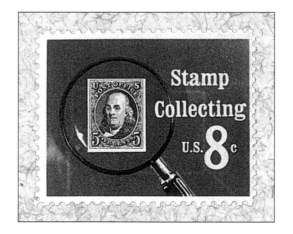

The Beginner's Guide to
STAMP
COLLECTING

NEILL GRANGER

NEW BURLINGTON BOOKS

A QUINTET BOOK

Published by New Burlington Books
6 Blundell Street
London N7 9BH

ISBN 1-85348-319-2

Reprinted 1994

This book was designed and produced by
Quintet Publishing Limited
6 Blundell Street
London N7 9BH

The author and publishers would like to thank
Stanley Gibbons Auctions, Stanley Gibbons Ltd. and
Stanley Gibbons Publications for the loan of materials
and transparencies used in this book.

Typeset in Great Britain by
Central Southern Typesetters, Eastbourne
Manufactured in Hong Kong by
Regent Publishing Services Limited
Printed in China by
Leefung-Asco Printers Limited

Contents

Introduction

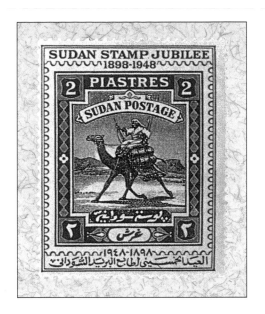

Ever since they were first invented, stamps have attracted the attention of anyone with a collector's instinct. In the early days, the aim was to save as many stamps as possible, regardless of their quality or variety, and to pack them into little bundles or save them in boxes. The Victorians made pictures out of stamps – rather like collages – or used them to cover screens. One of the most bizarre ideas was to make 'stamp snakes' by threading as many stamps as possible on a continuous thread – the longer the snake the better the collection!

As a hobby, stamp collecting is still as popular today as it was then but the approach has changed. Now, stamps are appreciated for the story each has to tell. The many designs that are used on stamps and the different countries they represent make them miniature windows to the world. Stamp collecting is enjoyed by enthusiasts of all ages and at all levels because it can be as easy or as complex as you want it to be.

At first, the fun part of this hobby is saving stamps from all over the world, particularly from obscure or far-away countries. Finding unusual items can often prompt a rewarding investigation into their origins and, of course, lead on to the next stage of stamp collecting. Whole new areas of history and geography (which may otherwise seem boring) come to life on these small, seemingly insignificant, pieces of paper.

In this book I have tried to lead you from first ideas about saving postage stamps towards beginning a specialized collection. There is information about buying and using the philatelic tools necessary to start a collection and useful initial guidance on some of the advanced aspects of philately. Basic know-how on valuing stamps and spotting forgeries or repairs is followed by some examples of spectacular varieties to whet your appetite. You could be lucky enough to buy one of these from your local post office – I was (see page 40).

Top of page and above:
Thematic collecting – displaying stamps appearing on stamps (see page 60).

History of
the Post

Although the first stamp was not introduced until 1840, the long and interesting history of postal services began in the seventeenth century. The postal service established in Great Britain also laid the foundations for similar post offices around the world, including America and Australia.

THE EARLY DAYS

Royal Beginnings

Originally, the only letters carried were those to and from the King and the royal court. The first public post was started in 1626, between London and Plymouth. Soon other postal services began and a network grew between the main cities. On 31 July, 1635 King Charles I issued a proclamation extending the use of the Royal Mail to the public.

The First Postmark

The Post Office was reorganized in 1660 and Henry Bishop was made Postmaster General. Bishop is remembered as the man who introduced the first postmark, first used in 1661. The Bishop mark, as it is called, only showed the day and the month of posting, and its purpose was to ensure that the letter carriers did not delay the mail. At this time all letters were taken to London, Edinburgh or Dublin before being sent to their destinations and Bishop marks were used in these cities, Edinburgh's being red. Similar postmarks were also used in America, notably in Philadelphia and New York, where they are called American Bishop marks or Franklin marks (after Benjamin Franklin, the Deputy Postmaster General).

Postal Rates and Routes

Early postal rates were very complicated. They were calculated on the distance travelled as well as on the number of sheets of paper included in the letter. The whole process was very time-consuming and expensive, so only businesses and the rich could afford to send letters.

A Bishop mark on the reverse of a letter sent to Great Witchingham, Norfolk, England, in 1693. It is interesting to note that the cost of postage was 7d (written on the front of the cover).

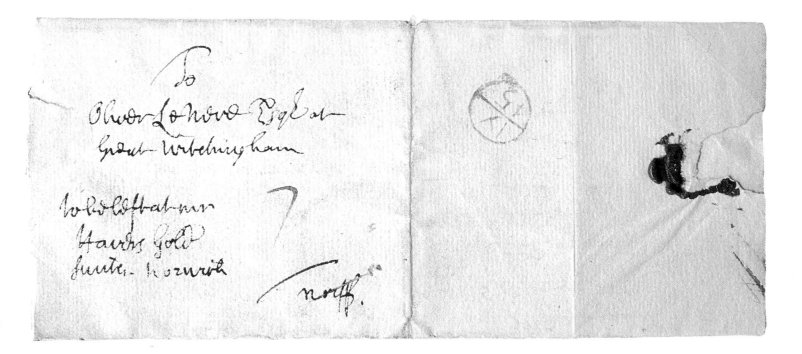

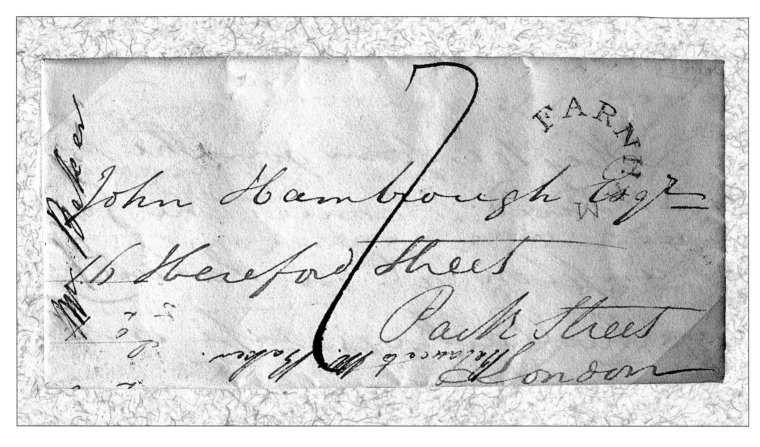

A typical town post-mark on a letter (top right) sent from Farnham to London in 1822.

Over the years there were many improvements to the postal system. At first, as I have said, all letters had to be carried to London, Edinburgh or Dublin to be forwarded on. There were six post roads around London and to improve this system, a series of additional routes was established which increased the network. Cross posts ran between two different post roads. By-posts ran between a post road and a town some distance from it. A way letter went between two towns on the same post road. Instructions were put on the bottom left corner of letters and you may see early covers with 'Cross post' or 'X-post' written on them.

Dockwra's Penny Post

A special local penny post was introduced in London in 1680 by William Dockwra. His service also introduced the first pre-payment of letters – the practice had previously been for the recipient to pay for the cost of the letter. This cheap local post was soon used in other major cities and was later adopted by many provincial towns.

The revenue from the postal service went to the Government. This London penny post was increased to twopence in 1801 to help finance the war against Napoleon.

Rowland Hill's Reforms

The man who pioneered the greatest postal reforms was Rowland Hill. His dream, which he was finally able to fulfil, was to have a cheap and efficient postal system which everybody could afford to use. He was also keen to introduce a convenient method of prepaying the postage and suggested 'a bit of paper just large enough to bear a stamp, and covered at the back with a glutinous wash'. He demonstrated that the cost of transporting a letter from one post town to another was almost negligible. He also showed that it would be far better to charge by weight rather than by the number of sheets. He suggested that there should be a uniform charge of one penny per half ounce made on all letters delivered within the United Kingdom and that payment could be prepaid by using a label or special stationery.

These recommendations were eventually approved. In 1839 a competition was organized for suggestions for types of adhesive labels and stamped paper. Although there were 2,600 entries, none was entirely suitable. The best of the ideas were refined by Rowland Hill himself, with the help of the printers Perkins, Bacon and Petch. However, the public demand for a uniform penny post was so great that the new rates were introduced on 10 January, 1840, months ahead of schedule and well before

One of the entries submitted for a competition to design the first stamp.

This cover, posted in 1815, shows the unpaid 2d mark. The letter, sent by local London post, was paid for by the recipient.

This envelope shows the postmark used for the penny post from Ipswich, Suffolk, England. A letter taken to the post office would be stamped instead of using one of the new penny black postage stamps.

any postage stamps were ready. Special handstamps had to be made for use by the post offices to indicate that the penny postage had been paid. Finally on 6 May, 1840 stamped wrappers designed by William Mulready and the famous Penny Black stamps were on sale at post offices.

offices. The twopenny stamp was not ready until 8 May.

It was thought that Mulready's stamped wrappers would be used most frequently. But the design was ridiculed by all and the penny and twopenny stamps were by far the most popular.

A Mulready envelope. This design was not popular and cartoonists of the time took pleasure in creating derogatory imitations.

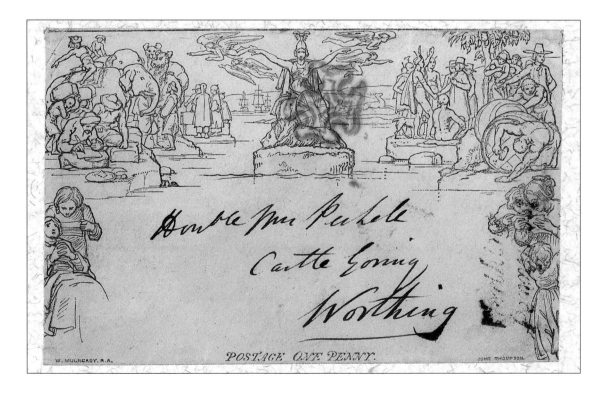

Early postal stationery.

POSTAL STATIONERY

When Rowland Hill invented the penny post he thought that the use of a stamped wrapper or envelope would become the normal method of sending a letter. He assumed that postage stamps would only be used occasionally. Of course, quite the opposite is now true and the use of postal stationery, other than registered envelopes, is rare today.

Postal stationery items have a stamp printed or embossed on them, so they are ready to be posted. There are several different types of postal stationery on sale, including the traditional selection of postcards, letter-cards, envelopes and registered envelopes. There are now some express services, such as Datapost or Skypack, which use special covers, but they are usually very large and are not popular with collectors.

United States of America, issued July 1, 1847.

Mauritius, issued September 21, 1847.

Bermuda, isssued 1848, and produced by the Postmaster, W B Perot.

Overseas Post Offices

After the issue of these first stamps, many of the British colonies expressed a wish to issue their own postage stamps. However, the General Post Office (GPO) in London dismissed this idea as it would be too confusing if more than one country were to use them. They believed that the postal workers would not be able to cope if hundreds of different postage stamps were available. So the first stamps which these colonies were allowed was a standard hand-stamp applied in red on letters. It showed a crown on top of a circle with the words PAID AT and the name of the city or country.

Other countries were not so restricted, and it was not long before adhesive stamps were appearing elsewhere. Brazil followed Great Britain on 1 August, 1843 with the issue of the famous 'Bull's Eye' stamps. The cantons (states) of Switzerland came next with their first issues in 1843 and 1845. These were followed by the United States of America and Mauritius in 1847 and France, Belgium and Bavaria in 1849.

Canada, issued April 23, 1851.

Russia, issued January 1, 1858.

British Guiana, issued July 1, 1850, and known as cotton reels.

Brazilian bull's eye, issued August 1, 1843.

India, issued April 1854.

New Brunswick, issued September 5, 1851.

New Zealand, issued July 18, 1855.

WEIRD AND WONDERFUL POSTAL METHODS

Sending a letter has not always meant popping it into a slot or box. Even within the last 50 years unusual methods of sending, moving and delivering mail have been used, particularly in remote parts of the world. Many local variations have been used since the tradition of sending mail began. Strange means of transport were employed to link more remote areas with the proper postal routes. For example, in the Australian bush a cyclist pedalled over a hundred miles with the mail. Rocket mail attempted to span rivers by attaching the letters and parcels to a rocket. Here are a few other examples.

ST HELENA STONE POST

St Helena is a remote island in the middle of the South Atlantic Ocean. Its position made it a good place for ships to stop and replenish their supplies of water. At the same time, they would drop off letters that had to be forwarded to other countries. Before the post office was opened in 1815, these letters would be left under special stones. The next ship to call would take any letters addressed to its country of destination onwards on their journey. It can be seen as a sort of haphazard postal junction!

TIN CAN MAIL

This method was mostly used in Tonga, a group of Pacific islands. Small boats carried the mail out to ships sealed in a tin can. Before this swimmers had made the risky journey from the islands out to the vessels.

BALLOON POST (BALLON MONTÉ)

This was a way of getting mail out of Paris when the city was under siege during the Franco-Prussian war between 1870 and 1871. Letters were sent soaring into the air in balloons. Of the 56 balloons that were floated out of the capital, 51 eventually reached the outside world.

RIVER POST

During the same siege, other desperate attempts to get mail out of Paris included sending it down the river in sealed canisters or metal balls. Many canisters were lost by this method.

Norway, issued January 1, 1855.

Ceylon, issued April 1, 1857.

Gambia, issued March 18, 1869.

What You Need to Start

This chapter explains what accessories are needed in order to begin a stamp collection. Even though there are only a few basic items of equipment, it is far better to start with the right ones than to think about new items as you progress – after all, you are laying the foundations of a good collection. First, there are notes about the different types of album, their particular advantages and disadvantages. Then the basic collectors' 'tools', such as hinges, tweezers, stock books and swap books, are listed and described. This will give you a good idea of what to buy as well as presents you may wish to receive for birthdays and Christmas!

ALBUMS

Although today we all think in terms of displaying stamp collections in albums, it used to be a common practice for collectors to sort their stamps into containers. A multitude of envelopes, old tins, chocolate boxes and other convenient containers were used to store them. I have even seen suitcases crammed full of matchboxes packed with different types of stamps. This may be a good way to start sorting out a few stamps, but it should only be a short-term method of keeping different groups apart. If you do not make the effort to transfer your stamps to an album, you may discover that you get quite hooked on sorting your whole collection into little packets, which is neither very convenient for looking at, nor for showing to other collectors and friends!

Why Use an Album?

To keep your stamps in good condition on a permanent basis, you must protect them from damage. Also, part of the enjoyment of collecting anything is to be able to arrange and display the items. This applies to stamps as much as to anything else, and you need an album to exhibit your collection. But why bother with an album rather than a scrapbook or an exercise book?

A proper album helps the philatelist to organize stamps neatly. Once they are placed in an album it is easy to see exactly what the collection contains or which other stamps you would like to add. Moreover, if you want to show your collection to others, or even to enjoy looking through it yourself, you will find that a printed album also gives some information about the stamps on each page.

There is a wide selection of albums from which to choose. They range from those costing a few pence to grand, leather-bound volumes. In a specialist stamp shop the choice may seem quite daunting, with shelves displaying many different kinds of albums, but they can be classified into a few basic groups.

Printed All-World Albums

These usually have fixed pages printed with large squares in which to place your stamps. They also have some illustrations of typical stamps from each country. This type of album is ideal for the new collector. If you are particularly enthusiastic you may consider looking for a loose-leaf album – they are usually much larger and more expensive but they are ideal for the ambitious philatelist.

A typical printed album. This one, with small squares, has illustrations at the top of the pages.

The three types of blank album:

spring-back

Find a container such as a box file, a small stout box (for example an old shoe box) or a large zip-up plastic folder to keep all your stamp-collecting equipment together. It is very easy – and particularly annoying – to lose hinges or tweezers and have to spend ages hunting for them when they are needed.

peg-fitting

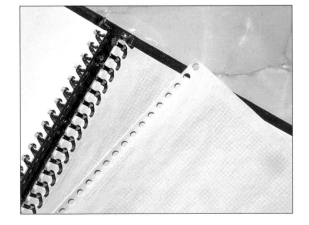

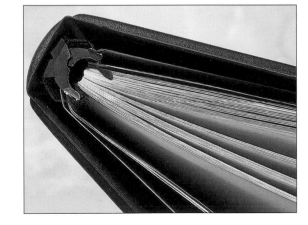

multi-ring

One-Country Albums

This is probably a second stage, as the hobby develops. If you decide to specialize by collecting the stamps of only one country, then this is the album for you. The pages are also printed with squares and helpful illustrations but they are loose-leaf so that pages may be moved. The printed squares do not cover the page completely in this type of album. Instead, they are grouped so that sets of stamps from the country are shown together. The value and description of each stamp may be printed near the empty square. Each year new blank pages are published for this type of album to hold current stamps or extra items which you have collected. You will find this album very useful if you want to collect just one example of each stamp issued by a particular country.

Blank Albums

These have pages printed with a faint background grid of small squares to help arrange the stamps evenly. They are always made up of loose leaves so that the positions of pages can be changed or new pages added as a collection develops.

Although these albums are used by specialist collectors, do not let that put you off using one as a beginner. The loose-leaf format is very useful for a general collection, which is likely to hold more stamps for one or two countries than for others, so more pages may be added where and when they are needed.

There are three types of blank album: spring-back albums, peg-fitting albums and ring or multi-ring albums. Spring-back albums are the most popular because they are not too expensive and they hold a good number of pages. The peg-fitting albums tend to cost more and include some of the best available.

Ring albums have the advantage of lying flat when they are opened, although in some types the pages do have a tendency to tear around the holes provided for the rings. If you happen to have a ring album remember to handle it carefully when turning the pages.

Do not worry at this stage if the album you can afford, or are given, is not quite as large as you hoped for, or not exactly the type you wanted. As your collection increases in size it will outgrow its first album anyway. Most collectors enjoy rearranging their stamps, and some people change their albums several times before they are happy with the way the stamps are displayed.

Blank loose-leaf albums are ideal for both specialists and beginners.

STOCK AND SWAP BOOKS

Stock and swop books. From pocket size upwards, a handy way to keep stamps on a temporary basis.

Once a collection is under way, the stamps probably have to be sorted out before they can be mounted in an album. Most collectors also want to have duplicate stamps, ready to swap. A stock book is ideal for both purposes. Made up of stiff pages, each with a series of plastic strips which are open at the top, a stock book holds stamps neatly in place. At the same time, they may be moved around easily. Although stock books come in a whole range of sizes, at this stage a pocket book is all you need. Of course, you could carry all your swaps around in an old envelope or small tin but the chances are that they will be damaged. Not only will a stock book protect the stamps, but you will be able to check quickly which spares you have or show potential swaps easily to a fellow collector.

STAMP HINGES

Mounting is the term used for sticking stamps in an album and using stamp hinges is still the best method of doing this. Hinges are now produced with peelable gum, which means that if you want to remove a mounted stamp, the hinge will peel off the back leaving a layer of gum on the stamp. Hinges are usually prefolded for greater convenience. Stamp hinges are very cheap, so do not be tempted to make do with either adhesive tape or glue!

Hinges. The most popular way to mount stamps. A packet like this will last a long time.

PLASTIC MOUNTS

The modern trend is to keep unused stamps with their gum untouched by a hinge – they are known as unmounted stamps. To display stamps in this way, plastic mounts are used instead of hinges. These are sold either in strips or cut to size and are commonly known as Hawid or Prinz mounts after the two major manufacturers. They are much more expensive than hinges, and although they are commonly used in specialist collections, I do not recommend them for a general collection because they can look very untidy when crammed close together in an album. You will find more information about different ways of displaying stamps and using plastic mounts on page 50.

TWEEZERS

Tweezers are used to lift or hold stamps. They help to protect them from being damaged by handling and, with practice, you will find it easier to pick up stamps with tweezers than with fingers. At first they may seem fiddly and unnecessary but it is a very good idea to get into the habit of using them.

Tweezers are available in either plastic or metal. The ends vary in shape – they may be spade-end, round-end or pointed. There is not a lot to choose between the different types, but I always feel that metal tweezers with round ends are the best – they do not have sharp edges or points that may accidentally damage the stamps.

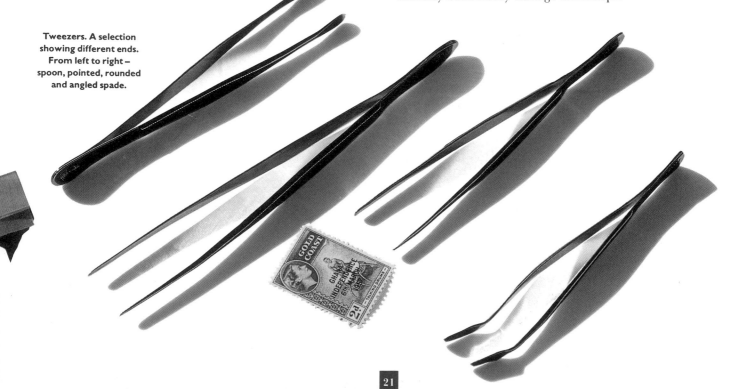

Tweezers. A selection showing different ends. From left to right – spoon, pointed, rounded and angled spade.

Stamps for Starters

The first stamps in any collection are probably going to be the ones off the mail received by family and friends. So make sure that they do not get thrown away by mistake. Tell as many friends and relatives as you can that you are collecting and ask them to save all their stamps for you, especially foreign ones.

At first, aim to collect as many stamps as you can find, from as many countries as possible. It is easy to get enthusiastic about examples from far-away places. It's also a good idea to buy a large packet of all-world stamps to get your collection off to a good start. Choose the biggest and most varied selection you can afford because the packet is unlikely to contain any stamps which you already own. Look out for these packets in stamp shops, stationers' or newsagents'. If the shops do not have anything to offer, buy a stamp magazine and read through the advertisements. You will almost certainly find packs of all-world stamps to buy by post.

Once you have mounted the first batch of stamps in your album, take care to avoid buying duplicates.

BUYING STAMPS

If you have time it can be a valuable exercise, as well as interesting, to look through what stamps are on offer and to decide which ones best fit into your collection. Discovering the scope of philately early on will help to highlight any specialized areas you particularly enjoy.

Packets of Stamps

You will find a wide variety of packets in the shops. They may contain stamps from all over the world or specialize in one country. Alternatively, some packets hold stamps with a common theme (see page 60). You will be able to see most, if not all, of the stamps that are included in the packet from the outside, so take time to choose the selection that interests you most.

Stamp packets come in a wide variety of styles.

Stamps on Paper

Stamp shops sell bags containing stamps still stuck to pieces of the original envelope on which they were posted. They are sold by weight, and are therefore known as kiloware bags.

The bags are usually filled with either stamps from your own country or foreign stamps. They will contain duplicates which you can hold as swaps. Sometimes there will be high-value stamps which ought to take pride of place in your collection.

Kiloware stamps are cheaper than packets, and they are ideal for bulking up a small collection. Before a bag of kiloware can be sorted, the stamps have to be soaked or floated off the paper, as explained on pages 47–8.

Starter Packs

These are for the very young collector who is just starting a collection. They contain some of the basic necessities such as a simple album, a packet of stamps, hinges and tweezers. Once you have become a 'serious collector', a starter pack is not a good choice – it is far better to select items separately to suit your requirements.

SWAPPING STAMPS

It is surprising just how quickly the enthusiast builds up a small stock of duplicate stamps. The rule is always to keep the best stamps for your collection and set the others aside in a swap book. Exchange these spares for stamps which are not in your collection. Remember that swapping should be a fair exchange. You cannot expect to swap a stamp in poor condition for a very fine one. Equally, make sure you get good stamps in exchange for your best swaps.

NEW ISSUES

A post office is the place to buy new stamps. Commemorative sets ought to be bought as they are issued, so it is a good idea to plan ahead and to note the dates when new stamps are to be released. The Post Office prints leaflets, sometimes with a calendar, listing dates when the new issues are due. Most sets are on sale for several weeks at main post offices, and for a shorter period at sub-post offices, where stocks do not last as long. Many people collect these sets on first-day covers (see page 63).

Kiloware – bags of fun for sorting.

FRAMA LABELS

For many years post offices have been using machines to dispense stamps to the public. Originally the machines sold stamps in coils or low-value booklets, but the fairly sudden increase in postal rates has made it more difficult for machines to provide stamps of useful values.

Multi-value machines are now used in a number of countries. These print the requested value on special labels, known as machine labels, automat stamps or Frama labels. The name 'Frama label' is taken from the Swiss company which made the first of these machines, which was introduced in Switzerland in 1976.

There has been a mixed reaction among collectors to these stamps or labels. Some people are avid collectors, but the majority still shun them. Frama labels are not widely used so keep any covers with them intact.

Frama labels on first-day covers.

WHAT ELSE DOES THE POST OFFICE OFFER?

The Post Office produces a large range of items for collectors, including presentation packs, postcards illustrating stamps and booklets, as well as unused definitive and commemorative stamps. Main post offices in some large towns have philatelic counters selling all the stamps and items produced for the special issues from the preceding year. If there is not a philatelic counter near your home, you can order back issues by writing to the Philatelic Bureau (see page 29). You can also write to the philatelic bureaux of overseas countries to buy their new issues.

FIRST–DAY COVERS

The Post Office sells special packs, postcards and envelopes for first-day covers. Shown here, a presentation pack to commemorate the wedding of Prince Andrew and Sarah Ferguson; a first day cover for the Year of the Child, a miniature sheet for the stamp exhibition in London in 1990.

STAMP SHOPS

As your collection grows you will have more reason to buy single stamps rather than relying on finding good examples in packets. This is when you need to know how to use a stamp shop. Unfortunately there are not as many stamp shops these days as there used to be. If you are lucky enough to have one near you, do not be afraid of going in – you do not have to spend large sums of money. As well as packets, kiloware bags and albums, most shops display individual stamps. They also display pages from old collections – usually each page is individually priced. Most shops have boxes of covers for customers to look through. The main stock of stamps is stored in albums behind the counter. Ask to see stamps of the country which interests you and the dealer will be happy to help and to answer questions, even though your purchases may be small.

Above and right: thematic collecting, butterflies on stamps (see page 60).

MAIL ORDER

If there is not a specialist shop nearby, you may have to buy stamps by post. Most shops offer a mail-order approval service. Stamps from a particular country or theme are mounted and priced in small books, known as approval books, which are sent to you to look through and to buy the ones you want. The approval book has to be returned by registered post along with the money for purchases. However, as you will be expected to pay for the postage both ways, as well as for the stamps bought, it can be expensive, especially for a new collector.

STAMP CLUBS

Ask at the local library for information on stamp clubs or philatelic societies in the area. Clubs usually have junior sections and joining one is an ideal way to meet other collectors. They are also a good place to pick up hints and tips as well as to find friends for swapping duplicates.

Most clubs run an exchange packet, which is similar to the dealer's approval service except that the books are made up by club members and the stamps are often much cheaper. With luck you will also be able to deliver the packet by hand to the next member on the list, saving on postage.

Stamp clubs hold regular meetings, with displays and talks by members or invited guests. Other events taking place throughout the year usually include an auction and competitions.

Entering the competitions can be a rewarding experience. Although they may seem mind-boggling at first, read the rules carefully and do not be afraid of making mistakes – nobody will mind. Many years ago, as an enthusiastic new member of the local stamp club, I entered three competitions. I had one entry in the thematic category, even though I did not know what a thematic collection was. Needless to say my entry came well and truly last because it was unsuitable, much to my embarrassment. However, as some consolation one of my other exhibits received favourable comments making the whole effort worthwhile. Remember: nothing ventured, nothing gained.

STAMP DEALERS

The term 'stamp dealers' is used for owners of stamp shops as well as for people who run small businesses from home. There are also a number who buy and sell on a mail-order basis. They provide a number of services in addition to offering lists of stamps which they have for sale, and many dealers include approval services and postal auctions. Check stamp magazines for addresses and details of services.

STAMP FAIRS

Stamp fairs are held at different venues all over the country and details are advertised in the local newspapers. They are usually

Stamps sunk at sea. The 'Leaping Tiger' stamp of the Federated Malay States (Negri Sembilan, Pahang, Perak and Selangor) is well known among philatelists for its many different values and corresponding colours. A delivery delay in 1922 resulted in a shortage of 4c stamps, so 5 million 3c stamps were overprinted with a 4c value. Before these surcharged 3c stamps were put into use, new supplies of the regular 4c arrived from the printers and, apart from samples supplied to officials, all of the overprinted 3c stamps were placed in weighted boxes and sunk in the sea.

held in a hotel or a church hall. The number of tables or stands where dealers will be selling their goods varies from fewer than a dozen to about 50 at the largest city-centre conventions.

Fairs are very useful for new collectors because many of the stands are run by spare-time dealers – philatelists who buy and sell stamps as a hobby and who therefore offer many bargains. These fairs are not held frequently so it is worth visiting any that take place in your area.

STAMP EXHIBITIONS

Stamp exhibitions are altogether grander than stamp fairs and they are usually well publicized. An entry fee is sometimes charged for this type of event. Many of the more important dealers take stands and there are displays of stamps which have been entered in the competitions organized specially for the exhibition. Allow enough time to have a good look round, as there are bound to be some bargains if you are patient enough to go through all the boxes of stamps.

Pay special attention to the displays of stamps. There may be some of particular relevance to your collection. Exhibitions are the ideal place to pick up useful tips, especially if you are thinking about specializing in any of the themes that are exhibited. Take note of the arrangement of stamps as well as the style of writing up. You may be able to incorporate some of the ideas in your collection.

AUCTIONS

Auctions are an established way of buying and selling stamps. There is a wide choice of auctions, from small events run by local dealers and clubs to the famous events run by international companies.

Stamps may be auctioned individually, in blocks, in sheets, as groups or even in boxfuls, and each is known as a 'lot'. All the lots included in the sale are described in

the auction catalogue with estimated selling prices, or values as given in general stamp catalogues such as those published by Stanley Gibbons and Scott. All the lots are available for examination – or viewing – before the sale and the details will be given in the auction catalogue.

Descriptions in auction catalogues vary considerably. Local sales are usually accompanied by catalogues giving only brief descriptions, as all the buyers will be present at the auction to view the lots which interest them. However, large international auction houses often sell to overseas bidders who do not have a chance to examine the stamps. Customers may well place their bids over the telephone or by post, so the details in the catalogue must be as full and as accurate as possible.

There is a wide selection of lots on offer, from individual stamps and covers to all-world collections. As your collection develops, you may consider buying a useful auction lot of all-world stamps. Remove the ones you want for your collection, then sell the remainder again – either offer them back through the same auction house, or sell them individually in the stamp club exchange packets.

Maximum cards (see page 90) showing stamp designs by artist Ralph Steadman. The set was produced to commemorate Halley's comet.

PHILATELIC BUREAUX AROUND THE WORLD

Buying new stamp issues from foreign countries is not easy. Some stamp dealers may have them on offer, but it is easier to write to the philatelic bureau of the country concerned. Some countries offer a standing-order service for philatelists, sending out each new issue of stamps when they become available. It is best to write asking for information first, then the bureau will send details of how to obtain the stamps. Here is a list of some international bureaux.

AUSTRALIA
Australia Post
Australia Stamp Bulletin
Locked Bag 8
South Melbourne
Vic 3205
Australia

BRUNEI DARUSSALAM
General Post Office
Philatelic Bureau
Bandar Seri Begawan 2050
Brunei Darussalam

CHINA
China National Stamp Corporation
Hepingmen
Beijing
China

CANADA
Philatelic Service
National Philatelic Centre
Canada Post Corporation
Antigonish
Nova Scotia B2G 2R8

CYPRUS
Philatelic Service
Department of Postal Services
Nicosia
Cyprus

DENMARK
Postens Fimaerkecenter
Vesterbrogade 67
DK-1620 København V.
Denmark

FINLAND
P&T of Finland
Postimerkkikeskus
POB 654
SF-00101 Helsinki
Finland

FRANCE
Service Philatelique
18 rue François-Bonvin
(F) 75758 PARIS cedex 15
France

GREAT BRITAIN
The British Philatelic Bureau
Edinburgh
EH3 0HN

GUERNSEY
Postal Headquarters
Guernsey
Channel Islands

HONG KONG
General Post Office
2 Connaught Place, Central
Hong Kong

ISRAEL
Ministry of Communications
Philatelic Services
12 Yerushalayim Blvd
61080 Tel Aviv-Yafo

ITALY
Direzione Generale Post e
Telecommunicazioni
Vendita Francubolli per Collezioni
1-00100 Rome

JERSEY
Jersey Philatelic Bureau
PO Box 304L
St Helier
Jersey
Channel Islands

KOREA
Korean Philatelic Center
CPO Box 5122
Seoul 100-651
Republic of Korea

MACAU
Macau General Post Office
Largo Do Senado
Macau

MALAYSIA
The Philatelic Bureau
Postal Headquarters
General Post Office
Dayabumi Complex
50670 Kuala Lumpur
Malaysia

MONACO
Office des Emissions
de Timbres-Poste
2 Avenue Saint-Michel
MC-98030 Monaco Cedex

NEW ZEALAND
Philatelic Bureau
New Zealand Post Ltd.
Private Bag
Wanganui
New Zealand

PAPUA NEW GUINEA
PNG Philatelic Bureau
PO Box 1
Boroko
Papua New Guinea

SAMOA
Philatelic Bureau
Chief Post Office
Apia
Western Samoa

SINGAPORE
Singapore Philatelic Bureau
Postal Services Group
Singapore Telecom
1 Killiney Road
Singapore 0923

SOLOMON ISLANDS
Philatelic Bureau
c/- GPO Honiara
Solomon Islands

SOUTH AFRICA
Philatelic Services
Private Bag and Intersapa
Private Bag X 505
0001 Pretoria
Republic of South Africa

SWEDEN
PFA
S-105 02 Stockholm
Sweden

SWITZERLAND
PTT Philatelic Office
CH-3030 Berne
Switzerland

THAILAND
Philatelic Division
The Communications Authority
of Thailand
Chaeng Watthana Road, Lak Si
Bangkok 10002
Thailand

UNITED NATIONS
United Nations Postal
Administration
United Nations
New York
NY 10017
USA
or
Administration postale des Nations
Unies à Genève Palais des Nations
CH-1211 Genève 10
Switzerland

UNITED STATES
U.S. Postal Service
Philatelic Sales Division
Washington D.C. 20265-9998

USSR
Mezhdunarodnaya Kniga
Moscow USSR

ZIMBABWE
Philatelic Bureau
Posts and Telecommunications
Corporation
P.O. Box 4220
Harare

To obtain information on a country which is not listed, try writing to the Philatelic Bureau in the country's capital.

About Your Stamps

As with any other area of collecting, the first step in building up a good philatelic album is to sort all your stamps properly. Organizing a batch of stamps is not a daunting task – on the contrary, it should be both interesting and enjoyable. At first most collectors simply sort their stamps into groups by country. This may seem straightforward, but you will probably come across some which do not obviously belong to any one country.

As the collection grows, you will have to be selective about which new stamps to save. You may also decide to try alternative ways of organizing them. This is when it becomes important to understand something about stamps, such as the way in which they are made, the reasons why they are used, various aspects of their use and the journeys they make. This chapter explains how to identify stamps and points out the different features to look for when sorting.

SORTING STAMPS

Starting from the very beginning, turn your unsorted stamps out on a table and begin by picking out those from the countries which you recognize, setting them aside in piles. Look at the stamps that are left unsorted and you may find some which have similarities, so group these together. Compare the writing on the stamps – the country's name may be in a foreign language or even in a foreign alphabet. If you find stamps with the same foreign words, then put them together. Then work through the list on page 35 until you find these names and the translations. Then they can be allocated to the correct countries.

If you do not want to put sorted stamps straight into your album, find some clean envelopes, write the name of the country in the top corner, and keep the stamps inside. This is the best way of keeping stamps if you do not have time to sort and arrange them properly. Remember that the aim at this first stage is to build up a useful stock

WHAT'S IN A STAMP?

Perforations

Reason for issue

Year of issue

Country of issue

Face value

Country name

Designer's name

Postmark

Printer's name

of stamps from which to pick out items to spend more time mounting and arranging in an album.

When you have more than one example of the same stamp, select the best one for your collection. This means choosing an undamaged stamp with the neatest post-mark. Set other duplicates aside in your swap book.

LOOKING AT YOUR STAMPS

Take a close look at any one stamp and you'll discover that there is much more to the design than just a pretty picture.

Country Name

It is not difficult to identify the origin of most stamps as the countries are often either printed in English or at least recognizable in the foreign language even if the spelling is not the same as in English. However, some countries print only their initials on stamps and these can be a problem until you learn some of them. The list below gives translations of the names of the most common countries that employ the A–Z alphabet and it includes some of the main initials used.

The hardest stamps to identify are those from countries which use completely different alphabets. But once you have a good batch of foreign stamps you will soon recognize the names of the main countries which use foreign alphabets. Check any unfamiliar names in the following list.

Do not wrap elastic bands around bundles of stamps or clip them together with paper clips. Both methods may damage the stamps.

Stamps are often hard to identify when different alphabets are used.

Taiwan

China

Japan

North Korea

IDENTIFYING STAMPS

Crete

Greece

Cyprus

Bulgaria

Serbia

Mongolia

Yugoslavia

USSR

Morocco

STAMPS WITHOUT COUNTRY NAMES

Turkey 1908 commemorating Granting of Constitution

G.B. 1940's testing label, these are known as 'poached eggs'.

– Iran 1876 complete sheet of four.

Bahrain 1974 War Tax label.

Turkey 1876 surcharge.

Indonesia 1966 postage due.

G.B. 1960's testing label used for testing coil vending machines.

No Name Stamps

Today, Great Britain is the only country allowed to issue stamps without a name or initials, but showing only the head of the Queen instead. This is in recognition of the fact that Great Britain issued the first postage stamps. However, before international postal regulations were generally accepted, quite a few countries printed stamps without putting any names or other means of identification on them. Stamps of this type are not particularly common but when they do appear they can be very difficult to identify. The selection shown here offers a guide to many of these stamps.

Face Value

This is the term used for the value of the stamp, usually the price printed on it. This is nearly always printed in figures and is therefore easy to read and understand. A few stamps from the Middle East have their values printed in Arabic figures. The following list shows the Arabic numerals with their Western equivalents.

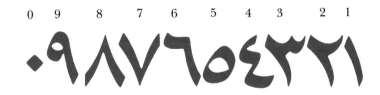

Usually the currency is also indicated, although some modern designs have abandoned the currency symbol. The majority of countries have changed their currencies at least once since they started issuing stamps and it is interesting to find examples of different currencies.

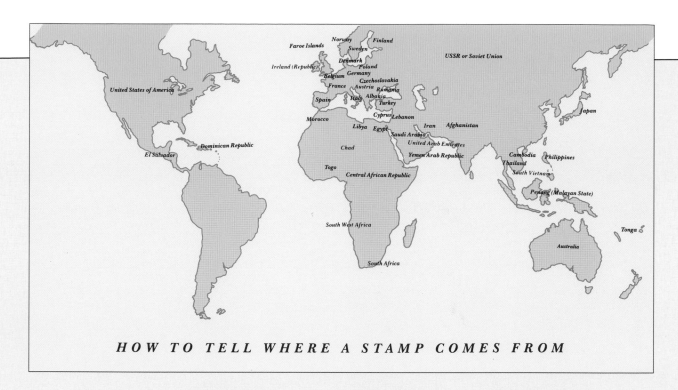

HOW TO TELL WHERE A STAMP COMES FROM

NAME ON STAMP	COUNTRY NAME	NAME ON STAMP	COUNTRY NAME
Afghanes	*Afghanistan*	*Osterreich*	*Austria*
Arabie Saoudite	*Saudi Arabia*	*Persia*	*Iran*
Bayern	*Bavaria (German State)*	*Pilipinas*	*Philippines*
België or Belgique	*Belgium*	*Polska*	*Poland*
Braunschweig	*Brunswick (German State)*	*Pulau Pinang*	*Penang (Malayan State)*
Cambodge	*Cambodia*	*Reichspost*	*Germany*
CCCP	*USSR or Soviet Union*	*RF*	*France*
Centrafricaine	*Central African Republic*	*Romana*	*Rumania*
Ceskoslovensko	*Czechoslovakia*	*RSA*	*South Africa*
Danmark	*Denmark*	*Rwandaise*	*Rwanda*
DDR	*East Germany*	*SA*	*Saudi Arabia*
Deutsche Bundespost	*West Germany*	*Sachsen*	*Saxony (German State)*
Deutsche Bundespost Berlin	*West Berlin*	*Salvador*	*El Salvador*
Deutsche Post or Reich	*Germany*	*Shqipëria (and similar)*	*Albania*
Dominicana	*Dominican Republic*	*Siam*	*Thailand*
Eesti	*Estonia*	*Suid Afrika*	*South Africa*
Egypte or Egyptienne	*Egypt*	*Suidwes Afrika*	*South West Africa*
Eire	*Ireland (Republic)*	*Suomi*	*Finland*
España or Española	*Spain*	*Sverige*	*Sweden*
Froyar	*Faroe Islands*	*SWA*	*South West Africa*
Français	*France*	*Tchad*	*Chad*
Grønland	*Greenland*	*Toga*	*Tonga*
Helvetia	*Switzerland*	*Togolaise*	*Togo*
Italia	*Italy*	*Türkiye*	*Turkey*
Jugoslovija	*Yugoslavia*	*UAE*	*United Arab Emirates*
Kibris	*Cyprus*	*UAR*	*Either Egypt or Syria*
KSA	*Saudi Arabia*	*USA*	*United States of America*
LAR	*Libya*	*Vaticane*	*Vatican City*
Liban or Libanaise	*Lebanon*	*Viet-nam Cong-Hoa*	*South Vietnam*
Magyar Posta	*Hungary*	*Viet-nam Dan Chu Cong Hoa*	*North Vietnam*
Maroc	*Morocco*	*YAR*	*Yemen Arab Republic*
Nippon	*Japan*	*Z. Afr. Republiek*	*Transvaal (South African State)*
Norge	*Norway*		

Unused and Used Stamps

Stamps which are saved off letters, parcels and packets have a postmark. They are therefore used stamps or in used condition. Stamps bought from a post office which have not been postmarked are unused stamps, or in mint condition.

It is not good practice to mix unused and used stamps randomly in a collection. When both types are displayed together on a page, take care to arrange them to best advantage, setting aside separate areas for both types.

Whether a collection is made up of unused or used stamps is a matter of taste. Some collectors are particularly interested in stamp design, in which case they do not want used items on which the designs are partly hidden by a postmark. Others prefer stamps with postmarks, to show that the stamps have served their intended purpose. Keen philatelists, well bitten by the stamp-collecting bug, usually prefer to compare examples of both.

Cancelled to Order

Some stamps appear to be used, with neat postmarks positioned across their corners but still with all the gum on the back. These stamps are called 'cancelled to order'. They have been postmarked by the postal authority, then sold at a discount price to stamp dealers. Postal authorities of some countries do this as a way of selling huge numbers of stamps in order to make more money. These stamps are exactly the same as those sold for posting letters, so they do have a place in your collection. However, it is much better to have a genuine used example if you have the choice.

Appendix Issues

Some countries produce dummy stamps for young collectors, called appendix issues. They feature colourful designs and can usually be recognized because the 'postmark' has been included as part of the printing process. These stamps also have all of their gum on the back. Although they are very pretty, these should not be included in your collection as they are not valid for posting letters.

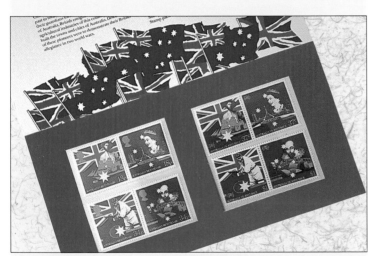

JOINT ISSUES

Occasionally, two countries get together to issue the same design on stamps. For example, for the Australian bicentenary, both Britain and Australia printed stamps which were based on the same design. The Soviet Union and America teamed up to produce stamps to celebrate the linking up of their Apollo and Soyuz spacecrafts.

Year of Issue

An increasing number of countries include the year of issue at the bottom of the stamp. You may be able to decide on the year that the stamp was issued by other clues, such as the design – for example if it marks a centenary or other special occasion. Knowing the year of issue can be very useful for organizing the stamps in chronological order in your album. It also helps if you are trying to find information about them in a stamp catalogue.

COMMEMORATIVES AND DEFINITIVES

There are two main groups of stamps, definitives and commemoratives.

DEFINITIVE STAMPS

These are the regular-issue stamps of a country, the ones that will be used for a number of years. They may either be small stamps, often showing the leader of the country, or they may be larger and pictorial. A pictorial issue (or group) of definitives usually consists of stamps with a similar design, showing different aspects of one theme related to the country. For example, sets of stamps may feature buildings or wildlife. Definitive stamps have to cover all the postal rates, so their face value ranges from the smallest unit of currency to high-value stamps for use on large parcels.

COMMEMORATIVE STAMPS

These are produced to mark important events or anniversaries. They are usually larger and more colourful than definitive stamps and the reason for issuing the set will be shown quite clearly in the design. Commemorative sets are often made up of between two and six stamps of different face values, although there are exceptions when just one or two values may be printed. As well as sheets of stamps, commemoratives are sometimes printed in blocks of sets, each surrounded by a margin, rather like a miniature sheet of stamps. These are produced especially for philatelists.

Printers and Designers

The names of the printers and artists or designers are sometimes included underneath the design on the stamp. Further information about specific stamps may be found in the post office literature or in stamp catalogues.

POSTMARKS

Postmarks are put on stamps to prevent them being used more than once and to provide a record of when and where a letter or package was posted. There is a variety of postmarks and they can be classified into three main groups.

Circular Date Stamps (c.d.s)

As the name implies, this is a circular postmark which shows the date of posting. It is applied by hand and it includes the name of the town or city around the outside with the date, and sometimes the time, in the centre. These are the neatest (and thus most prized) of the postmarks. Sometimes special-event postmarks are used, most commonly for cancelling first-day covers, and these include many elaborate designs.

Slogan and Machine Postmarks

These postmarks are made up of a circular date stamp with a statement, slogan or series of wavy lines to one side. For example, alongside the date stamp there may be a reminder to use the postcode or there may be a note about a special holiday location or national event. They are the most common type because they are used in automatic cancelling machines. The date stamp is usually on the left so that it is printed on the envelope itself and may be read easily. The slogan part of the cancellation will cover the postage stamp. These postmarks often obliterate much of the stamp and they can look quite ugly; avoid having them in your collection if you can.

Parcel Cancels

These are the heaviest postmarks used by the Post Office. Usually made with a large, oblong, rubber handstamp, they are designed to cancel several stamps at once and to work on difficult surfaces such as a parcel might present. These postmarks often obscure so much that the stamps are not worth collecting.

GUM

Until the late 1960s gum arabic was normally used on stamps. However, this shiny gum gave the stamps a tendency to curl, especially in hot and humid conditions.

Synthetic gums are now used, the most common being polyvinyl alcohol (PVA), which has a matt surface and is almost invisible. A tinge of yellow is often added to make the gum slightly visible on the stamps. One of the main advantages of synthetic gums is that they do not curl or discolour in hot climates, and sheets of stamps are less likely to stick together.

Self-adhesive stamps have been produced by several countries including Gibraltar, Sierra Leone and Tonga. These are sold on backing paper which is peeled off before the stamps are fixed to envelopes.

PAPER

Paper production is a complex and precise process. The selection of raw materials, the combination of additives and the methods used to make the paper are highly specialized. Just look around your home and you will find a wide variety of different types of paper – writing papers, books, packets, leaflets, magazines, newspapers etc. Stamps are printed on good-quality, fine, smooth paper.

Today, paper is made by machine, although small quantities of handmade paper are still produced and used or sold for special purposes. The following is a rough outline of the paper-making process.

Some typical company names printed on stamps. (see page 79)

(see page 79)

PICK OF THE POSTMARKS
The best stamps to collect are the neatest, usually the ones with a circular datestamp. However, the ideal postmark need not be the one which falls just across the corner of the stamp. Some collectors like to see as much of the postmark as possible to show that the stamp was used at the correct time for its date of issue. In fact in some collections the ideal stamp is one which has a light postmark perfectly centred on the stamp – commonly referred to as 'socked on the nose'.

It is made from vegetable fibre, mainly wood. Traditionally pulped rags, including linen and cotton, were used, along with straw and other fibrous materials such as esparto, a type of grass. The fibres are important as they play a major part in determining the quality of the paper. Different materials produce fibres that vary in length and size; therefore wood from selected species of trees is used.

Making Paper Pulp

The first stage is to reduce the raw materials to a pulp. This may be done by mechanical means or, more commonly, by using chemicals, either acid or alkaline depending on the materials used. The pulp is refined and improved by the addition of whitener, resin or size (gelatinous glues), clay, chalk or minerals. This ensures that the finished paper is of the high quality required for printing the details found on stamps. Phosphorescent materials are also added as they are required to activate automatic sorting machines.

Rolling, Draining and Drying

Once the exact mix of porridge-like pulp is achieved it goes through a process of draining and rolling by machine. The pulp is first drained down to fibres on a conveyor-belt system before being rolled. While the paper is still wet it passes over rollers

THE UNIVERSAL POSTAL UNION

On 9 October, 1874, at the end of a conference held in Berne, Switzerland, the General Postal Union was founded, with 22 countries as members. Austria – Hungary, Belgium, Denmark, Egypt, France, Germany, Great Britain, Greece, Italy, Luxembourg, the Netherlands, Norway, Portugal, Rumania, Russia, Serbia, Spain, Sweden, Switzerland, Turkey and the USA. The agreement between these countries meant that all post could travel freely between them without any charges made en route. It took a long time to reach this stage in the history of postal services and many previous attempts had floundered. For the first time these countries could send and receive post without having to count all the items of mail to find out how much they had to pay or collect in the way of international charges.

On 18 May, 1878, the name of this organization was changed to the Universal Postal Union (UPU). At the same time it was decided that all other countries should be encouraged to join. At the turn of the century, the majority of countries were members.

There have been various improvements and changes in this century, and the UPU still holds the same important position today as it did when it was founded.

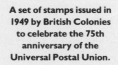

A set of stamps issued in 1949 by British Colonies to celebrate the 75th anniversary of the Universal Postal Union.

The same designs were employed for different countries, a process known as omnibus.

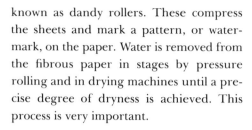

known as dandy rollers. These compress the sheets and mark a pattern, or watermark, on the paper. Water is removed from the fibrous paper in stages by pressure rolling and in drying machines until a precise degree of dryness is achieved. This process is very important.

Types of Paper

Stamps are printed on two main types of paper, known as wove and laid paper. Many other types have been used, but they are not common. Four other examples should be mentioned just in case you come across them. Chalky paper was used until recently, and granite paper is sometimes found on stamps issued at the beginning of the century. Batonné paper has a pattern of parallel lines set some distance apart running through it. Quadrillé has a pattern of lines set in squares.

WOVE PAPER

Wove paper is so named because it has a woven mark running through it. It is made by passing the 'raw' paper over dandy rolls which are covered in a wire which has a woven pattern, rather like a cloth. Most old stamps are printed on wove paper. If you hold an old stamp up to the light, then turn it slightly until it is at the correct angle to see the texture of the paper, you will just be able to see a plain, even woven pattern. This is similar to the pattern in the paper used for printing newspapers.

LAID PAPER

This type of paper has a pattern, or watermark, of parallel lines running close together through it. You will also find them in high-quality writing paper. You may have noticed that some writing paper is sold as laid paper.

CHALKY PAPER

This paper is coated before being used. This gives the stamp a shiny surface and the printing is much sharper. Modern paper coatings are not very obvious, but they can be recognized by the sharp quality of the printing.

GRANITE PAPER

This is a wove paper which also has coloured fibres in it. These fibres are easily visible on the back of the stamp.

WATERMARKS

A watermark is a pattern in the paper. Technically wove and laid are both types of watermark but the term is only used for a particular pattern produced at intervals in the paper. A watermark is pressed into the paper when it is made. Small metal stamps known as 'bits' are attached to the dandy rollers. These bits impress their pattern into the paper. The result is that the paper is slightly thinner in the watermark area and the impression can usually be seen by holding the stamp up to the light (see page 53).

The original reason for using a watermark on stamps was to make them more difficult to forge. These days printing methods are so advanced that it is far more difficult to make realistic forgeries of stamps, so watermarks are no longer important. Many countries have stopped using them, including Great Britain. A great variety of watermark designs have been used. Britain has used watermarks of crowns, anchors, orbs, national emblems and royal cyphers on stamps. Other countries have used an elephant's head (India), a swan (Western Australia), a lion (Norway), turtles (Tonga), a pineapple (Jamaica), a shell (Travancore), a horn (Norway and Holland), Basuto hats (Lesotho) plus numerous emblems, stars, letters and numbers.

A lucky find made soon after the stamps were issued. The two 1½p stamps shown include one (on the right) which is uncoated. The coated stamp has sharper printing.

PERFORATIONS

When the first stamps were issued they did not have perforations. Instead they had to be cut from the sheet with a pair of scissors – an inconvenient and time-consuming process. In the early years of stamp production which followed, there were numerous experiments to develop a way of easily separating single stamps from sheets. Eventually in the 1850s, Henry Archer invented a machine which made lines of holes around each stamp. He sold the patent for his perforating machine to the British Government and the first sheets of fully perforated stamps were put on sale in 1854.

Types of Perforation

The two main types of perforation are known as comb and line. They are made by two sets of sharp pins which pierce the paper from above and below. You may also come across pin perforations and roulettes.

COMB PERFORATIONS

Comb perforations are punched into the paper after the stamps have been printed. Modern perforating machines punch the horizontal and vertical holes at the same time. The perforations form a regular pattern around the stamps.

LINE PERFORATIONS

Older stamps had the horizontal and vertical perforations punched in two separate operations. These are called line perforations and they can be recognized by the fact the holes do not match perfectly at the corners of the stamp.

PIN PERFORATIONS

Instead of having perforations punched out, the holes are made by machines with only one set of sharp pins. The perforation marks are stamped from above but no paper is removed.

ROULETTES

Roulettes are cuts made between the stamps. They do not go right through the paper and none of the paper is removed. The most common roulette has small, straight

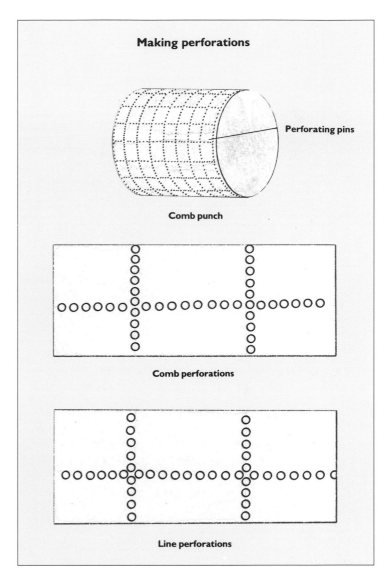

Making perforations

Perforating pins

Comb punch

Comb perforations

Line perforations

cuts around the frame of the stamp; sometimes the roulette teeth are inked by the printers and the stamps are said to be rouletted in colour. Other roulettes include a zigzag made up of short straight cuts marked at an angle in alternate directions. A serpentine roulette has the cuts marked in undulating wavy lines.

Measuring Perforations

Perforations are measured by the number of holes in a distance of 2 cm. They can easily be measured using a perforation gauge (see page 53).

1

**An essay for the King
George V Jubilee stamp.**

STAMPS IN THE MAKING

1 Today, stamps begin with a design from the artist. Reaching the final piece of colour artwork means going through many official decisions. Here's an example of an artist's painting for a 1935 King George V Silver Jubilee stamp. This one was drawn actual size, but complicated pictures are often drawn larger at this stage.

2 A die proof was an engraving of a design for printing on stamps produced by older methods. A proof would be printed from the finished engraving before the go-ahead was given for the stamps. This die proof would be checked for errors in the engraving. These are typical die proofs for a New Brunswick shilling stamp (1851) and one for a US Sanitary Fair stamp.

2

**Die proof for United
States Sanitary Fair
stamp.**

**Die proof for New
Brunswick shilling stamp.**

3 *Colour trials were samples used to decide on the actual colours which would be printed for each value of stamp in a set made up of the same design. These were examined and discussed by officials. Here are three examples of King Edward VII stamps, used in Kenya, Uganda and Tanganyika while they were known collectively as 'British Central Africa'. The centre trial was chosen for the 1a value but the others were not used.*

4 *Colour Separation. These samples show colour proofs for a set of stamps. Each proof is printed in one colour only. The proofs for each colour are checked for strength of colour and accuracy before the colours are combined in modern printing processes.*

King Edward VII stamps, used in Kenya, Uganda and Tanganyika.

3

A New Zealand miniature sheet designed to show the process of colour separation.

4

PRINTING METHODS

Although there are five basic methods of printing, modern printers mainly rely on the one known as photogravure. This is quick and cheap, and it can be used for printing many different colours.

Printing the first stamps was a skilful, very slow process in which the design was first engraved by hand on a special steel plate. It is worth knowing about the different methods which have been used so that they can be recognized on old stamps.

Line-Engraved or Recess Printing

For this method the design is cut, engraved or recessed into a metal plate known as the printing plate. The plate is covered with ink, then the surface is wiped, leaving the ink in the recesses. The plate is applied under pressure to slightly dampened paper so that the ink makes the best impression.

Recess printed stamps are easy to recognize. The printed area is made up of fine lines of ink which stand out from the paper. You may be able to feel the tiny ridges by carefully running the tip of one finger over the surface of the paper, but this is not always possible.

This is a relatively expensive method of printing, it does not show significant changes in tone and it is limited to the use of one or two colours. Therefore it is not widely used these days even though it is still thought to give the best-quality stamps.

Typographed (Typeset, Letterpress or Surface) Printing

This is the opposite of recessed printing. The design to be printed is raised above the surface of the printing plate. Rollers coated in ink are used to apply the ink to this raised surface. The design is then transferred to the paper by stamping it on. If you look carefully at the back of an unused stamp you should be able to make out small ridges, especially around the edges of the design.

This particular method of printing dominated stamp production from the 1850s until the 1930s.

Lithographed Printing

For this method, a flat printing plate is used and its surface is treated with special chemicals to create the shape of the design. The chemicals ensure that the ink only sticks to areas of the design to be printed. A comparison may be made with the way that ink will not adhere to a waxed surface. In the early days of stamp production some printers even used flat stones as the printing plate, producing some very crude results.

Offset lithography is a modern development of this printing technique. For this method the image is transferred from the plate to a rubber roller before being printed on the paper.

Photogravure (Rotogravure)

As I have said, this is the most usual method today because it is ideal for creating the detailed, multicoloured designs used on modern stamps. It is also fast and cheap.

If you use a strong magnifying glass to look closely at stamps printed by this method, you will see that the design is made up of many small coloured dots. If you look closely at pictures printed in a newspaper you will see the same effect.

The artist paints the picture to be used on the stamps in an enlarged form – usually about 15 cm (6 in) square for square stamps. The colour artwork is put through a special machine which produces a separate photographic image of each colour which has been drawn. This process is known as colour separation. Each of these colour images is then repeated side by side to make up a sheet. Each separate colour sheet is produced in the form of a fine screen which breaks the pattern into the tiny dots. This pattern of dots is etched on a copper print-

Some German propaganda forgeries were overprinted to suggest the demise of the British Empire. (Note that the cross on top of the crown is the Star of David.)

ing cylinder. To print the stamps, ink is spread over this cylinder and the surface is wiped before the design is transferred to the paper. The paper may pass through several different colour cylinders to complete the design of the stamp. This is similar to the recess printing method except that the etched dots are very shallow.

The machines print the sheets of stamps on large rolls of gummed paper, so the process is very fast.

Embossed Printing

The paper on which the stamps are printed is sandwiched between two plates. The design is recessed on one plate and raised on the other. This method is very slow and expensive, and is therefore rarely used. However, it was used for some stamped postal stationery until quite recently.

A modern variation of embossing is called blind embossing. Only the raised plate is used to highlight certain features, such as the Queen's head on British stamps.

Design Errors

Sometimes mistakes occur at the very first stage of making a stamp, when the artist draws the first design. Despite the fact that the picture on each stamp must be checked and approved many times before it ever reaches the printer, some errors have slipped through.

These stamps are fairly common as the error may well not be corrected in later printings. Sometimes it may be corrected when the stamp reprints, in which case it is a good idea to have an example of the 'before' and 'after' stamps in your collection.

Phosphor Bands and Coatings

There were a number of experiments in the late 1950s to try to develop a machine which would automatically sort envelopes so that the addressed side was uppermost. Having envelopes the right way up means that the postage stamps can be cancelled automatically and the mail is sorted more quickly. These machines are known as automatic letter facing machines.

One of the most successful machines used phosphorescent ink. This gives off a small amount of visible light for some time after being exposed to ultraviolet light. The ink was applied in bands to the sides of the stamps and these bands are known as phosphor lines. As mail went through the machine, it would recognize the phosphor lines on stamps and turn the envelope with that side facing up.

Phosphor bands are not always easy to see, especially on used stamps. If you hold the stamp up and tilt it at an angle so that light is reflected off the surface, you may notice that the phosphor lines are matt while the rest of the surface is shiny.

Recently stamps with phosphor bands have been replaced by others whose surface is completely covered with a phosphor ink. Alternatively, the phosphor may be included in either the paper or the coating.

Before phosphor stamps were introduced in Great Britain, experiments were done using black lines of material which conducted electricity. These thin vertical lines printed on the backs of stamps are known as graphite lines. They may be found on low-value stamps issued in 1957.

D E S I G N   E R R O R S

A St Kitts- Nevis stamp showing Christopher Colombus using a telescope, even though the telescope had not been invented during Colombus' lifetime.

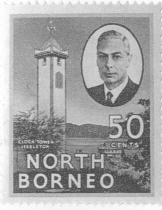

North Borneo 50c stamp, with a spelling error. Jesselton is the name of a town, shown incorrectly as 'Jessleton'.

A Fiji 1½d stamp, showing a boat without the boatman. This one was corrected.

Collectors' Techniques

It is important to learn the basic skills of stamp collecting, to ensure that your album gets off to the best possible start. It is also these techniques that will give you a good grounding for the future when dealing with more prestigious and possibly more valuable stamps. So do not dismiss basic advice such as how to handle stamps – this is exactly the sort of thing that should become automatic, so that there is no danger of damaging stamps by picking them up clumsily. This chapter also offers ideas for preparing and mounting stamps and advice on using a stamp catalogue and the other tools of the trade.

HANDLING STAMPS

Being small and difficult to handle, stamps are easily damaged. So one of the first rules of stamp collecting is to learn how to handle them. It is best to use tweezers whenever possible. They may seem a little awkward at first but using them will soon become second nature if you master the technique. I now find that I cannot value a collection without my tweezers in my right hand!

Using Tweezers

The best tweezers are those made of metal and with round ends. Make sure that there are no small bits of metal sticking out at the open end to damage your stamps. Tweezers should not be too stiff to use, as you do not need much pressure to hold a stamp firmly. If your tweezers are too stiff you should loosen them slightly. Squeeze them together at the end with the grip, just before the two pieces become joined at the handle. Hold the open end firmly in the other hand and flex the tweezers.

Using tweezers at all times will prevent your stamps from getting dirty and avoid fingerprint marks on the gum of mint stamps. Eventually you will find that it is also very much easier and quicker to sort stamps using tweezers.

Hold the tweezers about halfway along

Thematic collecting: trains on stamps (page 60), including an interesting example from New Zealand with a missing colour.

their length, not too near either end. To pick up a stamp, slide the lower lip of the tweezers under it. Until you are used to using tweezers, prevent the stamp from sliding away by gently steadying it with one finger of your other hand. Close the tweezers gently on the stamp so that you can lift it. Do not squeeze too hard.

Keeping Stamps Safe

Keep as many stamps as possible in either your albums or your stock books. Do not cram too many together into a stock book as they will have a tendency to fall out. Take particular care to avoid creasing the corners when placing stamps in a stock book. They can be kept safely sorted into packets, but take care when looking through to avoid damaging them and do not rummage for particular stamps – it is better to turn them out to see what is there.

REMOVING THE BACKING PAPER

Most stamps are printed with durable inks and immersing them in water will not harm them. However, some inks and coatings do react with water, so these stamps have to be floated off their backing paper. If you are uncertain about the types of inks and coatings used on a stamp, always float it off rather than soaking it off.

Soaking Off Stamps

Fill a bowl with water (or use the sink if possible). Put in all the stamps to be soaked off and gently stir them with your fingertips to ensure that they do not stick together. After about half an hour several will have come off their backing and sunk to the bottom. Have sheets of blotting paper or kitchen towel ready by the bowl. Take out the pieces of envelope. If any stamps remain attached they should come off easily. Bend the backing paper so that a corner of the stamp is free, then hold this corner gently and continue to bend off the backing paper.

Carefully place the stamp face down on top of the blotting paper and discard the unwanted paper.

When all the stamps are soaked off, lay another sheet of blotting paper on top of them and lightly press them. Let them dry thoroughly and keep them pressed under a book for a while to ensure that they stay flat. Because they have been thoroughly soaked, the gum should have been completely removed, so there is little danger of the stamps sticking to the blotting paper.

Be careful with stamps that are stuck on coloured envelopes, as the colour from the envelope often runs. It is very difficult to remove stamps from such paper without staining them. Always treat these stamps separately to avoid discolouring others which you are processing.

Floating Off Stamps

This technique is similar to soaking off, except that only the backing paper gets wet. Carefully float the stamps, face up, on the surface of the water. The time it takes for the water to soak through the backing will depend on the type of paper but several should be ready after 20–30 minutes. More care and patience is needed when using this method, as the gum will not be as soft as on stamps that are soaked off.

Lift the stamp and backing paper from the surface of the water, taking care to prevent any drips from falling on to other stamps. Bend the backing paper away from the stamp until a corner of the stamp is free. Hold this corner and gently bend away the rest of the backing paper. If the gum is still stuck too firmly for you to be sure of

Taking stamps off envelopes

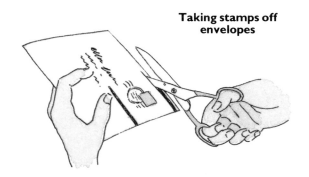

1 Cut neatly around the stamp – look out for interesting postmarks, which could be kept with one stamp.

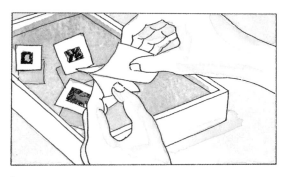

3 Using fingers, gently peel the paper from the stamp, not the other way round! (Tweezers can damage a wet stamp.)

2 Float stamps face up in a bowl of clean, tepid water for 20-30 minutes.

4 Put stamps between sheets of blotting paper, and leave to dry.

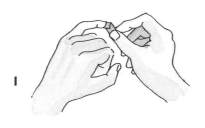

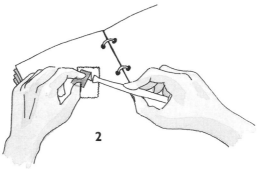

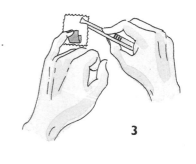

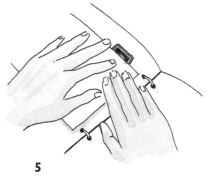

Using stamp hinges

1 Moisten the flap slightly.

2 Press moistened flap on to the back of the stamp.

3 Then moisten a strip across the bottom of the hinge.

4 Position stamp on the album page.

5 Put a sheet of clean paper over the stamp and press gently.

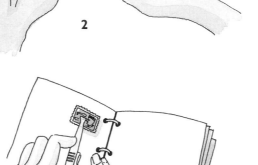

removing the stamp without tearing it, set it aside until all the other stamps have floated off properly. Then carefully float the half-stuck ones again.

Place the stamps face down on blotting paper. There will still be traces of gum on the back (even if it is not visible) so do not sandwich them between sheets of blotting paper. Either remove the gum by brushing it off with a fine, clean paintbrush and water, then place a second sheet of blotting paper on top, or just leave the stamps to dry. The second method leaves the stamps badly curled but they will soon flatten out when they are pressed in a stock book.

Some stamps require extra special care. Remove these from their backing paper by placing them on a wet flannel or a pad of wet kitchen paper, in a saucer.

MOUNTING THE STAMPS

Whether you use stamp hinges or plastic mounts depends on the type of album you have and the amount of money you are prepared to spend!

Using Stamp Hinges

These are usually ready folded for convenience. If they are not, fold over the top quarter with the gum on the outside of the fold. Lightly lick the smaller part of the fold and press this on the back of the stamp. Place the mount as near to the top of the stamp as possible, but without overlapping the perforations. When you have decided where to mount the stamp, lightly lick the larger portion of the hinge and carefully press the stamp in position. Make sure that it is in exactly the right place and that it is straight, then press it firmly with a piece of clean paper. If you have made a mistake, do not try to remove the stamp straight away – leave it for at least half an hour, or until the gum on the hinge is completely dry. Once the gum has dried the hinge will peel off the page without damaging the stamp. If the gum is still moist it is likely to leave an unsightly mark or, worse, damage the stamp.

The advantages of stamp hinges is that they are very cheap and easy to use, and they do not show at all.

Plastic Mounts

The fashion for mounting unused stamps so that they do not have the slightest hinge marks has led to the development of plastic mounts. These are very good for a more specialized collection where there are fewer stamps mounted on each page. When using plastic mounts it is very easy to swap stamps for better examples.

Plastic mounts have black or clear backgrounds and they are sold either cut to shape or in strips. If most of the stamps in a collection are similar in size, then it is convenient to buy mounts which are already cut to the correct size. Most collections, however, have some stamps that are an unusual shape or size, so it is a good idea to buy some strips of mounts. It is almost impossible to cut these mounts neatly with a pair of scissors, so it is best to buy a proper mount guillotine. A guillotine makes using mounts more expensive but it does save a lot of trouble. It also avoids ruining a lot of expensive mounts, which is enough to put the most enthusiastic philatelist off!

Plastic mounts are not suitable for a general collection in which all the stamps are placed side by side. They look very cumbersome in these arrangements and the mounts also tend to distract attention from the stamps. If you have a valuable stamp to which you do not want to attach a hinge, it is better to keep it separate from the main collection until you have a suitable album in which to display it.

If you are using plastic mounts, decide on the correct position to fix the mount in the album. Remove the stamp from the mount, then carefully lick the bottom of the mount. It is important to remove the stamp before licking the back as any moisture which finds its way between the two pieces of plastic can affect the gum on the stamp. This will leave areas of the gum highly glazed and reduce the value of the stamp. Moisten only the bottom 4 or 5 mm of the mount, as this makes it easier to make any small, final adjustments to its position.

Use tweezers to place the bottom edge of the mount in exactly the right position, then press it down firmly. If you need to replace the mount in the future, it will be possible to remove it from the album page without causing too much damage.

ARRANGING STAMPS IN YOUR ALBUM

The first challenge when arranging a general collection is to make it look interesting. Notes and ideas on more specialized collections are discussed in greater detail in the next chapter.

Damaged stamps or ones which have heavy postmarks should not be included permanently in a collection. If they are important to the collection, they may be put in position until a replacement can be found. Aim to change any for a better example as soon as possible.

Planning the Page

Before beginning to stick any stamps or mounts, work out how to group the stamps on the pages. There is little point in starting at the top left square and working across and then down the page, as this will only show the order in which the stamps were collected. Instead, group similar stamps together; for example, place definitives at the top of the page with the commemoratives below. Try to separate the used stamps from those that are unused. When displaying different stamps from the same set, arrange them in order according to their value.

However they are organized, stamps should be mounted carefully, in neat, straight lines. They should sit squarely on the page and not overlap their neighbours.

Moving Stamps and Thinking Ahead

Remember that it is very easy to move items mounted with stamp hinges, so there is

Thematic collecting: ships on stamps (see page 60), here showing the development of sea travel from clipper ships, steam ships, ocean liners and more modern battleships.

nothing to stop you from rearranging the stamps several times. Do not worry about leaving gaps on pages, either to separate groups of stamps or to allow you to insert stamps which you hope to find or buy in the future. Make a list of stamps which you particularly want to add to a collection.

STAMP CATALOGUES

Stamp catalogues are price lists or guides. They are published by leading stamp dealers around the world, including Stanley Gibbons (UK), Scott (USA), Michel (Germany), Yvert & Tellier (France), and Sassone (Italy). Catalogues cover different areas of philately. The standard type is an all-world catalogue which covers the basic stamps issued by all countries. An all-world catalogue does not usually give information on variations in the stamps (different watermarks, shades of colour etc).

Main dealers in all countries publish specialized catalogues of home stamps as well as all-world catalogues. For example, Stanley Gibbons publish a Great Britain catalogue; Scott publish a United States catalogue; Campbell Patterson publish a New Zealand catalogue; and Seven Seas Stamps publish an Australian catalogue.

Apart from Great Britain, most of the above catalogues are one-volume publications. The Great Britain catalogue is published in five volumes but there are less detailed versions available in one volume. In addition, Stanley Gibbons publish a series of catalogues covering all countries, each one giving more details than the all-world catalogue.

As well as providing a guide to the value of stamps, a catalogue offers a wealth of information. All catalogues include a general section about stamps, their watermarks, their perforations and other details. Always read the information on how to use the catalogue, since the layout is often a little difficult to follow, and each company has minor variations in presentation.

Using a Catalogue

Here is a quick guide to using a catalogue. At the front there is an index or contents list where relevant. The contents are in A–Z order by country or in chronological order – the order in which the stamps were issued. Other systems may be used in more specialized catalogues.

To find a stamp look up the country, then look up the year of issue, and then look down the list of stamps issued in that year to find the item.

If you do not know the year of issue then look at other stamps which are illustrated from that country. Look for those with pictures of the same ruler or with a similar style of illustration. Catalogues usually illustrate one stamp from each set or series. Once you have found the series, simply read down the list to find the particular stamp.

There are two colums of prices printed in catalogues. The column on the left is for unused stamps and the one on the right is for used stamps. Remember that these prices are the selling prices of that dealer's stock, and are for stamps in perfect condition. A guide to estimating the value of your stamps against the value in the catalogue is given on page **52**.

For each issue the catalogue gives the title of the set, the date of issue and the face value of each stamp in the set. There is often also information about watermarks, perforations, colours, printers, printing methods and designers.

USING A CATALOGUE

Below: An annotated catalogue entry, featuring the British Christmas card series (catalogue numbers S.G. 1414–8), accompanied by the stamps (below right) as you might buy them.

Right: The rare error of value was due to an increase in postal rates during the production of this issue. A few stamps with 13p (instead of 14p) slipped out.

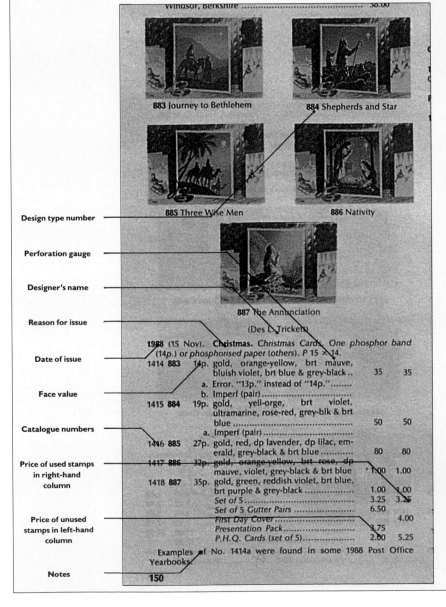

Windsor, Berkshire 6.00

883 Journey to Bethlehem

884 Shepherds and Star

885 Three Wise Men

886 Nativity

887 The Annunciation

(Des L. Trickett)

1988 (15 Nov). **Christmas.** *Christmas Cards. One phosphor band (14p.) or phosphorised paper (others). P 15 × 14.*

1414	883	14p. gold, orange-yellow, brt mauve, bluish violet, brt blue & grey-black ..	35	35
		a. Error. "13p." instead of "14p."		
		b. Imperf (pair)		
1415	884	19p. gold, yell-orge, brt violet, ultramarine, rose-red, grey-blk & brt blue	50	50
		a. Imperf (pair)		
1416	885	27p. gold, red, dp lavender, dp lilac, emerald, grey-black & brt blue	80	80
1417	886	32p. gold, orange-yellow, brt rose, dp mauve, violet, grey-black & brt blue	1.00	1.00
1418	887	35p. gold, green, reddish violet, brt blue, brt purple & grey-black	1.00	1.00
		Set of 5	3.25	3.25
		Set of 5 Gutter Pairs	6.50	
		First Day Cover		4.00
		Presentation Pack	3.75	
		P.H.Q. Cards (set of 5)	2.60	5.25

Examples of No. 1414a were found in some 1988 Post Office Yearbooks.

150

Design type number

Perforation gauge

Designer's name

Reason for issue

Date of issue

Face value

Catalogue numbers

Price of used stamps in right-hand column

Price of unused stamps in left-hand column

Notes

WATERMARK DETECTORS

The simplest way of looking at the watermark is either to hold the stamp up to the light or to place it face down on a dark surface. There are also a number of detectors to use for looking at watermarks which are difficult to see.

Lighter Fluid

Place the stamp face down in a small black or dark-coloured tray, or use a sturdy lid from a jar. Squirt lighter fuel, as used in wick-type lighters, over the stamp, using just enough to cover it. The watermark should show up quite clearly. Use tweezers to remove the stamp from the tray and blow on it until it is dry.

This method is not often used nowadays but it does have the advantage of revealing any repairs, creases and other faults as well as the watermark; moreover, it does not damage the stamp.

Morley Bright Detector

This detector works on the principle that the paper is thinner at the watermark. A thin, sealed plastic sachet containing dark ink is placed over the stamp and pressure is applied evenly over it. The ink spreads but remains most dense where the paper thins on the watermark, and the impression of the watermark shows up.

Sinoscope

This works on the same principle as the Morley Bright detector. The stamp is placed between two clear plastic plates which are held together under pressure and a light is shone on to the stamp. This highlights the thin area of the watermark. Be aware, however, that a sinoscope is an expensive piece of equipment.

Older types of detector used coloured filters to pick up watermarks, but they were not very successful and are not easy to find today.

MEASURING PERFORATIONS

Perforations are made around stamps so that they can be torn easily from the sheet. If the holes are too close together, the sheets will tear too easily. If the holes are too far apart, individual stamps may tear when they are removed from the sheet. The printer tries to balance these two extremes and decides on the size of perforation which is best suited to the paper.

A set of stamps may be issued with more than one size of perforation. For example, different printing companies may have been used during the life of the issue and different printers have different perforating machines or two machines may have been used because of a breakdown.

Perforation Gauges

Perforations are measured by the number of holes in 2 cm. There are two basic types of perforation gauge. The first has a selection of differently spaced dots printed on a card or plastic surface within a 2 cm mea-

Using a Morley Bright watermark detector – when it is closed and opened again, the impression of the watermark will show on the right, on the plastic-sealed inkpad.

A range of magnifying glasses including a microscope type (bottom).

sure. Most gauges have perforation measures ranging from 7 to 18 per 2 cm. The stamp is placed on top of the measure and the perforations are compared to the dots to find the best fit. This type of gauge is probably the easier of the two to use.

The second type has a grid of lines printed on a clear plastic rule. These lines are graduated in terms of the distance between them. The rule is placed over the stamp and moved until the lines on the gauge exactly match the perforation points on the stamp. The measure is then read at the side of the scale. These gauges are not particularly difficult to use, and they give a precise reading.

The gauge is adjusted until the lines fall exactly on the teeth of the stamp and the perforation measurement can then be read.

MAGNIFYING GLASSES

A magnifying glass is often thought of as an essential piece of equipment for stamp collectors, second only to a pair of tweezers. This is not really true, however, especially for beginners.

Consider what you might need a magnifying glass for before deciding to buy one. Sometimes there are small figures or numbers included in the design of the stamp. These show which printing plate the stamp came from. The best-known stamps with these numbers are the British penny plate number stamps issued between 1858 and 1879. On these stamps the plate number is engraved in each margin of the design. Many of the numbers can be read with the naked eye but some are quite difficult to see, so a magnifying glass is needed.

Some collectors also like to look for minor printing varieties – flaws or dots – which are repeated on sheets of stamps. These are called 'fly speck' varieties and can be found listed in specialized catalogues. As they are very small a magnifying glass is used to spot them.

As a professional stamp valuer, I also use my glass to examine stamps in detail, looking for any signs of forgery or to spot any stamps which have been repaired.

A magnifying glass is therefore only used to examine small details in the printing. As it is not an essential piece of equipment for a beginner, there is no point in buying a cheap glass which may give a distorted image. It is better to wait and to buy one of reasonable quality if you decide that you need one.

Opinion varies as to the best size. In my opinion, the ideal magnifying glass provides a magnification of 10 times and has a lens of 1½ – 2 cm diameter. This gives adequate magnification and the lens is big enough to avoid having to squint through the glass.

There is a wide choice of magnifying glasses available and it is worth visiting several shops – and not necessarily stamp shops. My glass was originally intended for examining geological specimens!

COLOUR GUIDES

Sometimes the same stamp is listed in the catalogue with two or more shades. It may be difficult to relate the colours listed to the stamp being examined, especially if you have only one stamp as an example. A colour guide, or colour key, shows patches (or swatches) of the basic colour types on a card, and can be matched to a stamp to decide on the exact shade which was used in printing.

Using a Colour Guide

Make sure that you are sitting in a good light. It is best to sit near a window in daylight but away from direct sunlight. Artificial light is not ideal for checking colours as it can distort the true colour of the stamp. Place the stamp on a clean piece of white paper. Hold the colour guide so that it overlaps the stamp slightly. Compare two or three shades until you decide on the closest match.

A colour key, a fan of colour shades to match against stamps.

Developing Your Collection

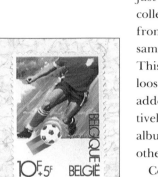

As your collection grows you will find certain countries or certain types of stamp more interesting than others. This soon becomes obvious when some album pages are full to overflowing while others have just a few examples. At this stage, most collectors decide to concentrate on stamps from one or two countries, while at the same time continuing to collect others. This means putting all your stamps in a loose-leaf album, so that pages can be added for the main countries. Alternatively, the stamps can be put in separate albums, one for the general collection and others for specific areas of interest.

Collecting by country is not the only way of organizing your stamps. There is a wide variety of themes on which a collection may be based, from butterflies and fish to space and aeroplanes. In this type of collection – known as a thematic collection – all the stamps have a pictorial connection with the chosen subject. Often the theme may be the principal reason for the design of the issue.

CONDITION: THE IMPORTANCE OF BEING SELECTIVE

It is important that all the stamps in your collection should be in the best possible condition. They should be clean, attractive and without faults. As you become more experienced, and when you try to sell or swap stamps, you will appreciate the importance of this. So it is best to start off with this in mind, otherwise the stamps acquired at first will soon be substandard by comparison to the rest of the collection. Check the following:

★ Perforations should be complete, with no slightly short perforations or blunt corners. Imperforate stamps (stamps without perforations) should have large, even margins.

★ Stamps should not have any thin patches in the paper or creases. Creased corner perforations which can be folded over easily should be counted as creases.

**Thematic collecting: sport on stamps (page 60),
showing here the most famous sporting occasion.**

Thematic collecting: animals on stamps (page 60).

★ The design should be well centred on the stamp.

★ Unused stamps should be unmounted, if possible, or lightly mounted. (Note that in most catalogues the price quoted for unused stamps issued after 1940 is for unmounted examples.)

★ Used stamps should have a neat circular date stamp. Whether this is central or across a corner is a matter of personal preference.

★ Covers ought to be in clean condition with good strikes (or impressions) of the postmarks.

SINGLE-COUNTRY COLLECTIONS

A single-country collection may contain stamps from your own country or a particular foreign country. Usually, when collectors first begin a single-country collection, they save all the stamps they find or buy from that country. This soon results in a large collection which may be improved by becoming more specialized.

For example, some people (the majority, in fact) decide to collect only unused stamps while others concentrate on only used stamps. Of course there are collections which combine both. It is also not unusual for a philatelist to limit a collection to just one example of each stamp of one country – this means that blocks, strips or varieties are not included.

Which Album?

This type of collection can be kept in either a special printed album or in a plain loose-leaf one. The choice depends on the content of the collection.

If the collection is going to contain one example of each stamp, then a special printed album is ideal. In this type the layout of the stamps is already planned and the collector concentrates on filling the gaps on the pages.

SINGLE COUNTRY COLLECTIONS

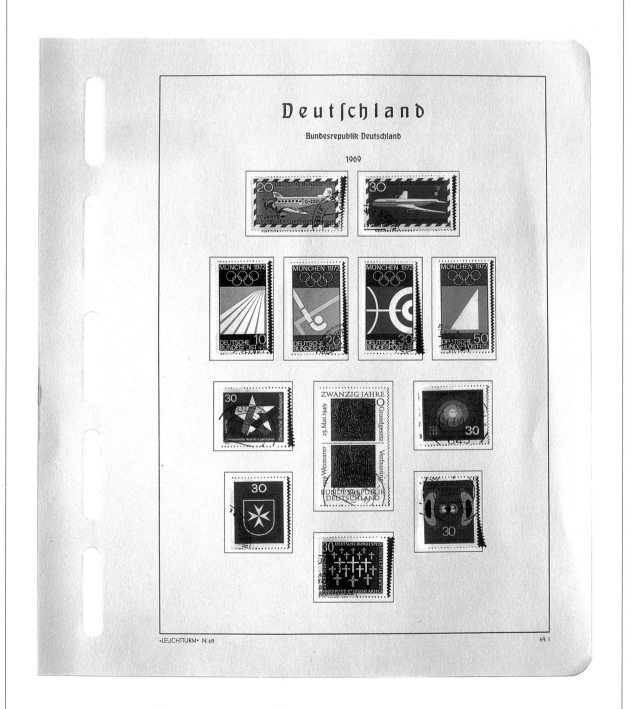

**A page from a single country collection, displayed on a page from a printed album,
using pre-printed stamp boxes.**

Thematic collecting: planes on stamps, these ones showing both military and civil planes.

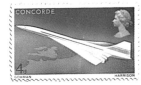

These albums also show which stamps have been issued by the country in each set, so the collector knows exactly what to look for. They are very popular, and ideal if you want to start a single-country collection as well as a main specialized collection. The information on the year of issue and face value of the stamps is all printed on the pages, so there is not usually enough space for adding extra notes. If you want to include different items in your collection, and enjoy finding out about the various sets of stamps that have been issued, the printed album is a bit limiting.

The most versatile choice of album is one with blank pages. These have the advantage of being cheaper than printed albums, and allowing the collection to develop or grow exactly as you want it to, with room for as much detail as you may want to add. More information on arranging stamps is given on page 69.

COLLECTING BY THEME

Many collectors find certain topics featured on stamps are particularly interesting to collect. Instead of looking for stamps from particular countries, they seek out any stamp which illustrates the chosen theme. It may be birds, animals, flowers, sport, space transport or perhaps a less popular subject such as food and produce. This way of collecting is called thematic or topical collecting and it is becoming increasingly popular. There are a large number of publications (magazines as well as books) devoted to thematic collections and to particular themes.

Organizing a Thematic Collection

Perhaps the most difficult part of thematic collecting is deciding on the best way to arrange the stamps in your album.

One method is to group together all the stamps which feature some aspect of the theme. For example, in a collection of birds on stamps, the stamps may be grouped according to the species of bird. This is one of the best ways of including background information about the subject but the pages often look unbalanced because sets of stamps have to be separated and completely different designs end up mixed on a page.

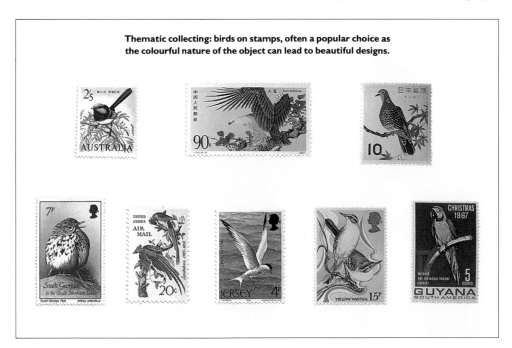

Thematic collecting: birds on stamps, often a popular choice as the colourful nature of the object can lead to beautiful designs.

Different sized stamps and even different printing methods are mixed together.

The alternative approach is to collect the stamps in the sets as they were issued. They should be arranged in A–Z order according to the name of the country in which they were issued. For each country the stamps should be organized in chronological order of date of issue. This is not the only method but it does show off the stamps well.

If you want to make up your own system, then try to keep sets of stamps together, as this makes for a better collection.

Including Background Information

Although well-organized stamps make the collection more attractive to look at, they cause problems with the presentation of the background information. Thematic collections combine information on the stamps with notes about the theme. For example, a thematic collection on space would include notes on the history of space travel. A set of stamps issued to mark an important space voyage would always be accompanied by written details of the voyage – the date, astronauts, etc. A collection on birds would include notes on the different species of birds. Since the same species would probably feature on many different stamps, it could be difficult to decide exactly where in the collection to put all the information about that species. This is all part of the challenge of developing a good stamp collection, and it can be interesting as well as enjoyable.

What Else to Include

Traditionally, a thematic collection would only contain stamps, but it is now acceptable, and far more interesting, to include covers, postcards and any other postal items which expand on the chosen subject. Only items which clearly display the theme of the collection should be used, however. It is very boring, when looking at a thematic collection, to have to spend time trying to understand the connection between the theme and the stamps or other items which are included. For example, a stamp showing a design with just a tiny bird in the background (or worse a few feathers!) will not fit into a collection on birds.

Thematic collecting: fish on stamps, from tropical waters to European rivers.

Thematic collecting: space on stamps, an ever popular modern theme with exciting new developments always being commemorated.

BOOKLETS

Booklets were first introduced at the beginning of the century. They were intended to be a convenient way of buying and carrying stamps. At first a small premium was charged to cover the cost of producing these booklets but it was not long before advertising was introduced to pay for this extra expense.

The first booklets were usually made up of panes of six stamps either stitched or stapled together with interleaving pages between stiff outer covers. Today most booklets are simply a folded cover with a block of stamps fixed by its margin. Quite often the stamps are of different values so that they add up to a convenient sale price for the booklet.

Many countries, such as Australia, Britain,

Canada, Singapore and Sweden, produce stamp booklets, sometimes for special occasions, sometimes for permanent sale. The booklets illustrated here show how the designs have changed and developed, from small, practical designs to large and exciting examples which may included labels and written information as well as stamps.

If there is space in your album, include some books in the unopened packet along with others opened out to show their contents. Use photograph corner mounts to keep them in place. Since they can take up a lot of space you may only want to show one or two as a special feature. Booklet albums are available, or you can use a plain scrapbook.

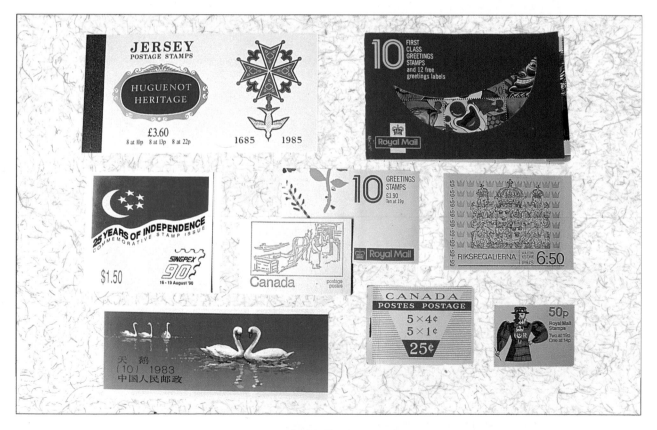

Examples of colourful booklets from all over the world.

COLLECTING COVERS AND POSTMARKS

A cover is an envelope or wrapper which has been stamped and posted. First-day covers are the most readily available and probably the most popular, but this is not the limit of this area of philately. Just as some collectors specialize by saving certain types of stamps, so others look for specific types of cover. Popular covers include those which have been damaged during transit. For example, the envelope may have been ripped in a sorting machine. Some covers may have been damaged by flood or fire. Older covers may have been rescued from wrecked ships; others may even have been saved from airline crashes.

Collecting crash covers is a subject in its own right, and involves covers from either airline crashes or boat wrecks. Less morbid topics that make some covers particularly interesting include decorative illustrations and interesting postmarks that indicate that the item travelled by an obscure route. Collecting by country is also comparatively easy for the beginner.

First-Day Covers

First-day covers are the most common. These are envelopes with a whole set of stamps on them, posted on the first day of issue. Special envelopes can be bought at a post office or from a dealer. On the day when the new set is released, a complete set is carefully stuck on to the envelope and it is posted in a special box at a post office. These stamps are cancelled with a commemorative postmark. The advantage of collecting first-day covers is that each envelope shows a complete set of the new stamps. The envelope also includes a special design to match the stamps. A card with printed background information is sometimes put in the envelope.

It is difficult to collect first-day covers in the same album as stamps so it is better to buy a special album. First-day cover albums have plastic folders instead of pages. Each folder is divided in half and has a black backing paper to display the covers to best advantage. Most albums are designed to mount four covers to each page. There are half-size cover albums which only hold two covers per page.

A typical first-day cover – this example is from South West Africa (Namibia).

Other Covers

Other envelopes with stamps, which may be decorative or particularly interesting, may be displayed with other stamps in an album, taking care to position them so that they tie in with the sets of stamps. Older covers are often collected alongside stamps as they highlight unusual and historical aspects of the postal service.

It is important not to litter a stamp collection with too many covers; those that you display should be really good.

What to Look For on Covers

Many of the interesting markings found on old covers may still be used today, with slight changes. Look out for any cover which has an unusual postmark, handstamp or label applied to it. For example, you may find postage due marks (also called tax marks); or marks giving reasons for delayed delivery; or covers which have been damaged in the post and stamped with an official mark to explain what has happened.

When collecting covers, not only is the condition of the envelope important but the postmark must also be of good quality. It is important to distinguish between covers which have been posted especially for collectors and those which have been 'commercially used', that is used by companies or for genuine correspondence.

Because of changes in postal rates it was, and still is, often necessary to make up the correct postage with more than one stamp. Covers of this type from the last century and the beginning of this, are collectable. It is unusual to find stamps of three different values on one cover (called 'three-colour frankings'), and such covers are held in esteem by collectors.

Mounting Covers

To mount covers in an album, it is best to use large photograph corners – two are usually sufficient. Take care when putting a mount on the same corner as the postage

MODERN COLLECTIBLE COVERS

A registered envelope from Germany to London, sent in 1864, this shows a good range of registered and other postmarks. Note that PD means 'paid to destination'.

A crash cover salvaged from an aircraft which crashed in Singapore in 1954 on its journey from New Zealand to England (note the burn and water stains).

This cover shows a rare postmark – an Amoy postmark used on Hong Kong stamps – which increases its value from being good to spectacular – British post offices in China and Japan used stamps from Hong Kong.

Interesting and collectable markings on modern covers showing Retour (return to sender), delay due to AIRCRAFT HIJACKED, insufficient postage for transmission by Air Mail, damaged in the post and postage due handstamp.

A credit mark on a letter sent in 1866 from Liverpool to Mauritius. The 4½d handstamp indicates the postage credited to Mauritius for delivery.

A letter from America, undelivered and returned to sender due to a postage strike.

stamps as it can catch and damage the corner of the perforations. Most covers look better if they are surrounded by a thin black border. This can be made by cutting a piece of black paper a little larger than the cover and placing it under it before fixing both to the album page. Alternatively, a black line can be drawn around the cover. Fix it to the album page and carefully make pencil marks just outside the four corners. Remove the cover from the mounts to avoid damaging it and draw a black outline with either a broad felt-tip pen or a draughtman's pen.

Picture Postcards

Old picture postcards may also be collected. The most popular subject to collect are cards which feature your home town, called topographic cards. It is always interesting to see how familiar streets and landmarks have changed over the years.

Cards can also be found which show social history including any subject featuring ways of life at the time, such as farming, schools or shop fronts. Many modern cards which are collectable feature old advertising posters, and these make an ideal subject.

Looking at Postmarks

Postmarks serve two purposes. First, they cancel the stamps and prevent them from being used more than once. Secondly, they show when and where the letter was posted. Sometimes there is more than one postmark on a letter. The cover may be stamped at various stages during its journey and these marks are called transit marks. Other postmarks may pass on information to the post-office staff or to the person who receives the mail.

Types of Cancellation

Postmarks are made by hand or by machine. In most countries ordinary mail is stamped by machine. In some small, remote places letters are still stamped by hand. Machine cancellations are usually in two parts. The first is a circular or square section with the date and town. The second is a series of wavy lines or a slogan (see page 38).

Picture postcards showing a poster reproduction (top), a street scene (middle) and a shop front (bottom).

Hand Cancellations are used in small offices without machines or on special letters and packets. Registered mail, special delivery and some express mail is stamped by hand. A hand cancellation is almost always round (although there are some oval ones), with the date and name of the post office (see page 12).

Transit Marks

These are usually found on old covers. Transit marks show the route that the letter or package took from when it was posted to when it was delivered. Today, the mail usually goes straight from one place to another with only one postmark. Before the worldwide postal system was this well organized, a letter could visit several places on an international route. At each 'stop' it would be stamped. This was not just an international characteristic. Even within one country a piece of mail could pass through several offices and receive a postmark at each stage. More commonly, it received first a despatch postmark then an arrival postmark at its destination. Working out the route from some old postmarks can be quite interesting.

Instructional Marks

These are usually only put on mail when there is something wrong. For example, a postage due mark is used if there is something to pay (see the feature box below). When a letter has to be returned, or if it is misdirected, then instructional marks are stamped on the envelope to send it on its way again.

**Top: Modern covers showing different postage due handstamps.
Bottom: A cover sent in 1863 from Manchester to York where it was re-addressed to Harrogate. Additional postage wasn't paid, and therefore a 1d postage due handstamp has been applied.**

POSTAGE DUES

Before postage stamps were used, the cost of sending a letter could be paid by either the sender or the recipient, usually the latter. In order to make the Penny Post work efficiently, prepayment became compulsory. Any unpaid letters were fined at double the normal postage rate and the amount to be collected became known as postage due. This system has been changed a little in recent years and it is now usual for a fixed surcharge to be added to the amount underpaid.

If a letter was redirected to a different address, then the postage had to be paid again. This is the reason why some unusual combinations of stamps are found on some nineteenth-century covers. This is no longer necessary and letters may be readdressed without surcharge.

To make the postal system run more efficiently all the member countries of the Universal Postal Union have come to an agreement by which the amount due on underpaid letters is collected by the post office in the country of delivery.

A set of advertising labels issued by J Coleman Ltd.

ADVERTISING

Postal authorities sometimes supplemented their income by selling advertising space. As we have seen, booklets are an ideal place for advertisements.

During the last century advertising on covers was much more elaborate and attractive, so much so that some envelopes were covered with illustrations, leaving only a small space for the name and address. The craftsmanship of early examples has made them quite valuable now. More recent examples are simpler and are often quite reasonably priced.

A booklet pane advertising Esso tyres.

An illustrated cover advertising Kardov flour.

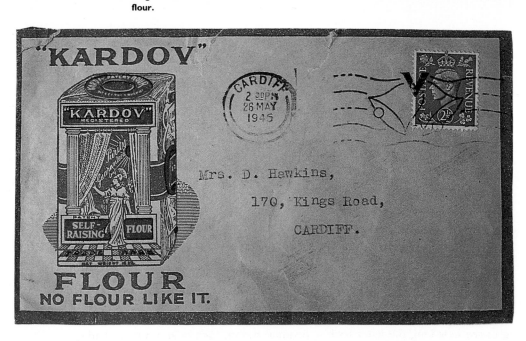

POST OFFICES ABROAD

In the middle of the last century, the major European powers of Britain, France, Germany and Russia had many interests in the major trading centres throughout the world. Some of these outposts were unable to use their stamps for overseas postage. So the trading nations each developed their own postal service for delivery of letters in and out of the city. These postal services are particularly common in the eastern Mediterranean and along the Chinese coast. Some important cities had services for all four countries.

Typical and commemorative Victorian postmarks (below).

A Brief History of Postmarks

The most interesting period for postmarks is the 1800s. Many countries were underdeveloped and their transport systems limited. There were fewer post offices then, so it is relatively easy to collect an example of a nineteenth-century postmark from each post office in a particular country.

The first postmarks often did not have anything to show which post office they were from. Later, numbers or letters were set in parallel bars or in circles. These were followed by the circular date stamps (see page 38), which are still used today.

Collectors now pay more attention to all the postal markings which are to be found on covers. At one time only the cost of sending the letter was important, as it changed quite frequently and could vary for covers sent to different countries. Even the route by which a cover was sent affected the cost. Up to the end of the last century international transport was slow and it was common practice to send two copies of important letters by different routes to ensure that at least one arrived as soon as possible. These early covers usually had a number of transit postmarks and it is interesting to see how long the letter took to travel between the different places.

WRITING UP AND ARRANGING A COLLECTION

In a specialized collection there are usually fewer stamps on each page and some information should be given beside the stamps. A large set of stamps can require a page on its own. Sometimes two small sets may be placed on the same page, but they should be clearly separated.

A Balanced Display

When displaying a few stamps on plain pages it is important to arrange them symmetrically. The page should be balanced vertically and horizontally. It is not necessary to arrange the stamps in strict value order, although they are better done this way. Consider the different ways in which the set (or sets) can be grouped on the page so that they look neat. Also allow room for writing notes which make the page more interesting. There are few sets which are easy to arrange in a square or rectangular pattern, so you will probably have rows of different lengths. Place the shorter rows at the top and bottom of the page with the widest in the centre. A regular pattern of this shape looks pleasing.

Adding Written Information

The written notes about each set should be included near the relevant stamps. Remember that the information on the page should given anyone looking at the collection a better understanding of the stamps. What, and how much, to write is, to some extent, up to you. It is usual to include the name of the set as a heading at the top of the page. The date of issue plus details of the watermark, perforations, printers and printing method used should be put beneath the heading, near the top of the page.

Notes about special features on an individual stamp, such as an unusual shade, should be written immediately below that stamp. Any extra snippets about the whole set, such as why it was issued or the number of sets printed, may be written below the stamps or at the foot of the page.

Try not to add too much in the way of information – remember that these notes are meant to increase interest in the stamps and not to overpower them. This is especially important in a thematic collection where the background information can easily dominate the page.

Although it may seem boring to spend so much time organizing the first page, it is well worth the effort as it sets the style for the rest of your collection. The last thing you want is to get halfway through writing up your collection and then decide on a better method of combining stamps and notes.

A collection which is made up of pages that are all written up differently will look very messy. Follow some of the suggestions illustrated on page 70–1 if you do not want to spend too much time developing your own style at first.

Finding Information

Although the main stamp catalogues will contain most of the information you need, you can borrow specialized books and catalogues from the local library if you want to add more detail. They usually have at least a small section on philately, and if you cannot find anything, then do ask an assistant before giving up. Most local stamp clubs also have their own libraries and are always keen to help new collectors. If all else fails, ask a local stamp dealer for information or write to one of the major dealers.

In this way you will at least learn more about the subject even if you do not find any wonderful notes to include in your collection.

Choosing a Medium for Writing Up

The majority of collections are written up by hand using a pen and ink but there are other ways that can look equally good.

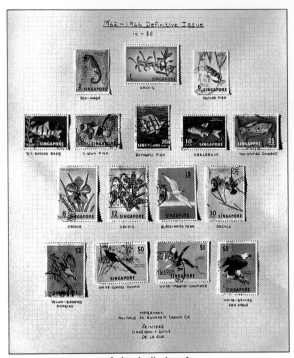

A simple display of Singapore stamps with essential handwritten notes.

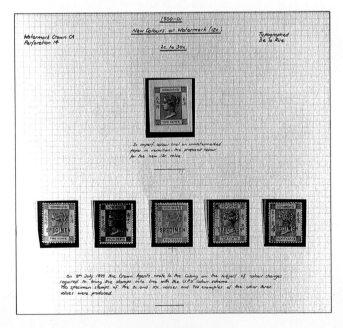

A page from a specialized Hong Kong collection, annotated with a draughtsman's pen.

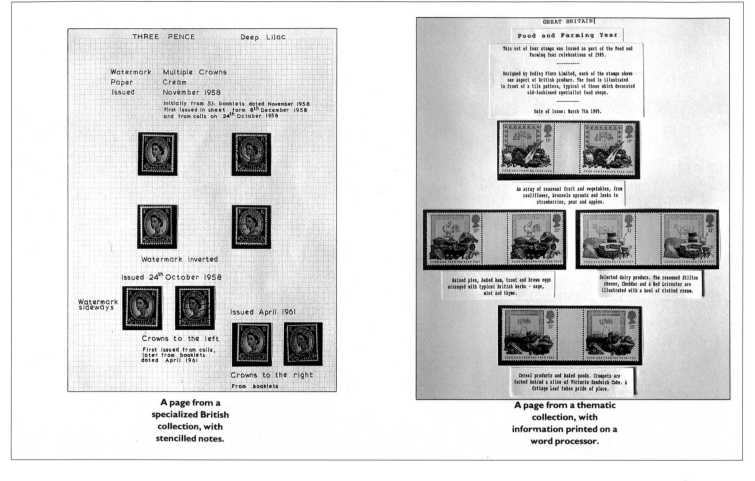

A page from a specialized British collection, with stencilled notes.

A page from a thematic collection, with information printed on a word processor.

A Pen

Choose a pen with a fine nib. There are several different types which can be used – a fountain pen, a draughtsman's pen or fine-point, felt-tip pen. Do not use a ball-point pen.

Time spent practising and developing your writing is well worth while. Italic writing can look impressive if it is all neat and even. To discover different ways of writing, borrow a book on calligraphy (writing methods and styles) from the library.

A Stencil Set

Small stencil sets are available from art shops. Use one of these to make all the letters exactly the same size. Again, practise using stencils first because it is difficult to space the letters evenly and neatly. It is also very easy to make spelling mistakes when using a stencil set.

Rub-On Lettering

Characters printed on special backing sheets ready to rub on paper (for example Lettraset) may be bought from art shops and some stationers, but they are expensive. I would not recommend them as the sheets contain the whole alphabet, while you tend to use only some of the letters. As a result, you will find that you always run out of the same characters.

A Typewriter

For a long time typewritten notes were thought to be very inferior and messy. However, modern typewriters and word processors are now often able to print compressed or micro lettering which is more suitable for use on album pages. Type or print notes in small sections on blank paper, then cut them out and stick them on the album page.

Colour and Illustration

All notes should be written in black. Serious philatelists frown on blue and other colours, which is worth thinking about if you ever enter competitions. Fine red lines used to underline headings will enhance the page, but other colours will detract from the stamps.

Including illustrations of varieties or postmarks will make the collection more interesting. Unless you are a good artist, however, practise drawing on neat pieces of paper as mistakes on an album page will ruin the collection. Stick the illustrations in place when you are happy that they are correct, clear, and the best you can achieve. Small, neat maps may also be used to make a collection look attractive and more interesting, especially with light colouring.

Valuing
Your
Stamps

Many collectors think that their stamps are worth the full catalogue value. Sadly, these ideas are shattered when their collections are professionally valued. This disappointment stems from a misunderstanding of the basis of catalogue values. By knowing exactly what the stamp catalogue's price means it is possible to put the value of particular stamps, and the whole collection, into perspective. As well as giving some idea of how to go about valuing a stamp collection, this chapter includes some information on the reasons why some stamps are valuable.

CATALOGUE VALUES

The values given in a stamp catalogue represent the prices of stamps in perfect condition when sold by the publishers of the catalogue. Stamps which are not in absolutely perfect condition will not be sold for the catalogue price. The majority of dealers and stamp shops sell their stamps at a discount on catalogue prices, often between 50 and 75 per cent of the catalogue value. This may seem a bargain but generally it reflects the quality of the stamps they are selling.

Guaranteed Quality

Although it is possible to find a bargain in small shops and through cheaper dealers, if you are spending a significant amount of money on a stamp, then you should be sure that the quality is guaranteed by buying through one of the main philatelic dealers. Stamps sold through these sources are valued by professionals. Less experienced valuers may well miss certain small defects which drastically reduce the value of a stamp, and which may not be obvious to collectors. Since the whole point of paying more to a major philatelic dealer is to guarantee the quality, you will not cause any offence if you check the stamp first. Read through the dealer's catalogue to see if there is a guarantee of quality.

VALUING YOUR OWN STAMPS

Every collector wants to be able to place a value on their collection, and you can do so without the expense of having a professional valuation. However, although it is relatively easy to arrive at an approximate value, there are many different factors which affect the precise figure and it is easy, and quite natural, to overestimate.

Valuing a Collection

To value a complete collection, ignore all stamps with the minimum catalogue value – this figure represents a handling charge and not the value of the stamp. Then ignore any that are in poor condition and any that you know are forgeries. Add up the catalogue value of all the remaining stamps and divide the figure by 10. This is the approximate value of your collection, and depending on the nature of the collection, it is unlikely to be greater than double what a professional valuation would produce, and, in fact, it could even be a little on the low side.

The quality and percentage value of imperforate stamps as listed in a catalogue (better examples will exceed the catalogue value)

From left to right:

Badly cut into the right-hand side: 10%

Large margins and neat postmark but just cut into the bottom right corner: 25%

Good postmark but cut close at bottom: 50%

Good margins but the postmark is not clear: 75%

Clean and fine with good-to-large margins: 100%

Valuing Single Stamps

This is much more difficult as so much depends on condition, where the stamp is to be sold and the demand for it at the time of selling. Assuming that the stamp is in perfect condition and that the market has not suddenly been flooded with examples, the approximate selling price should be about 25 per cent of the catalogue value. If it is sold by auction, the price should be higher – about 30–40 per cent of the catalogue price.

The following are a few of the factors that reduce the value of a stamp:

★ A hinge stuck on a unused stamp.
★ An untidy postmark on a used example, which could halve the value.
★ A creased corner or short perforation, which could mean that it is worth less than a quarter of the above value.
★ A thin area, tear or other serious imperfection in the paper, which will reduce its value to about a tenth of the value of an undamaged example.

REPRINTS

Stamp collecting has flourished as a hobby ever since stamps were first introduced, and soon after the first ones were issued there was a great demand for examples of the early issues of each country. In order to satisfy this demand a few countries printed further supplies of these stamps from the original plates specially for collectors. These are called reprints.

To the experienced eye reprints are usually quite easy to distinguish from the originals because they were printed about 20 or 30 years after the originals. The paper is often of much better quality than that used for the originals, the colours are brighter and the gum is smooth and glossy. As these reprints were produced only for collectors, very few have been lost and they are fairly common, especially in older albums. Unless you have handled the origi-

nals, it is easy to mistake a reprinted stamp for a genuine one and think it is valuable. Most catalogues have notes indicating which stamps have been reprinted but unfortunately these notes are not always comprehensive. If in doubt, assume the stamp is a reprint and seek an expert opinion.

FORGERIES

There are two main catagories of forgery: those produced to deceive the Post Office (postal forgeries) and those made to deceive collectors.

Postal Forgeries

Postal Forgeries are scarce and usually fetch high prices, especially if they are found on their original envelopes. One of the most famous examples of this type of forgery was used in the telegraph office of the London Stock Exchange in 1872. It was a very clever deception which went unnoticed at the time. The forger printed a passable likeness of the current shilling stamp, and gave a supply to an accomplice

Top: A proof of a 2s brown stamp forgery produced by Sperati.
Middle: A lithographed forgery produced by the Sperati method.
Bottom: A genuine 2s stamp.

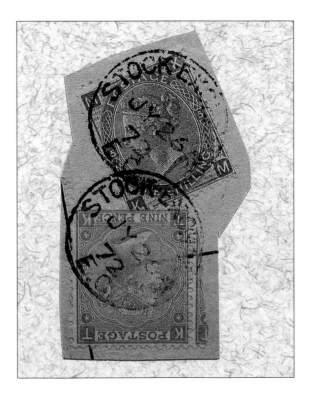

This Stock Exchange forgery is used on a parcel telegram form with a genuine 9d stamp.

Overprint forgeries on British stamps. Clockwise from top left: 1. genuine overprint; 2. lithographed forgery; 3. forged overprint on a stamp which was issued a date later than the genuine use of overprint shown; 4. very crude forgery; 5. genuine overprint; 6. a lithograph forgery with the overprint in an incorrect position.

to know. The clever part of this swindle was that the telegraph receipts never left the telegraph office, except for filing, until they were destroyed. It is not known how much money was stolen from the Post Office as the deception was not noticed until a famous dealer purchased a quantity of old telegram forms from the post office in 1898 and noticed some of the forgeries – 26 years after the original deception.

Forgeries Aimed at Collectors

Forgers producing stamps to fool collectors employ a wide range of skills in their art, although the modern forger concentrates more on repairing or faking overprints rather than producing stamps.

Some of the older forgeries are easy to detect – they were crudely printed and postmarked, and were made as space-fillers for collectors. Recent examples of this kind of reproduction are unlikely to deceive as they have the word FACSIMILE printed on the back.

The serious forgeries most often found in this category are those with forged overprints or surcharges. The forger takes a genuine stamp and applies a new overprint to make it appear to be a far more valuable variety. The quality of these overprints varies greatly: some are obviously wrong when compared to a genuine stamp, while others are dangerously good and can fool many experts. So be very wary of stamps with overprints which make them more valuable than those that are not overprinted.

who worked on the telegraph counter. Hundreds of telegrams were sent from the Stock Exchange at this time and it was easy for the counter clerk to use examples of the forged stamps on the telegrams and pocket the money. As long as his books balanced at the end of the day, nobody was

A comparison between crude forgeries and genuine stamps of Hong Kong and St Lucia.

British Intelligence produced many propaganda forgeries. This design, based on the German definitive, includes the inscription 'Futschesreich', meaning 'collapsed empire'.

A Famous Forger

Some very clever forgers will go to great lengths to perfect their art. The most famous stamp forger was Jean Sperati. He set out to make fools of those who set themselves up as experts by faking stamps which they would pass as genuine. First he would photograph a genuine unused stamp and prepare a printing plate. Then he took a used example of a cheap stamp and bleached out the colour of the printing, leaving only the postmark. The design of the valuable stamp was then printed on this. The result is a stamp on genuine water-marked paper and with a genuine post-mark. Sperati's skill was so great that his stamps easily fooled the experts.

Propaganda forgery produced by Germany and showing a broken battleship over Churchill's head.

Propaganda Forgeries

Warring nations frequently used propaganda to demoralize the enemy and to encourage their own troops. Stamps have also been used in this way, and many forgeries were produced during the Second World War. Both the British and the Germans produced stamps and cards which made fun of the opponents' leaders. These designs were usually based in the stamps used at the time and a lot of imagination and flair was exhibited by both sides.

IMPROVED AND REPAIRED STAMPS

Although this book is not intended to show in detail how enhancing stamps can increase their value, it is important to know what to look for.

Repairs

Tears can be stuck together again with a small amount of glue and only a small mark remains. A stamp without perforations may have a paper margin added by carefully building up a paper pulp around it, pressing and cutting it. These can be detected by close examination of the edge of the stamp. The missing parts are skilfully painted in and the join is sometimes visible. Missing corners can be rebuilt and thin areas in the paper can also be filled.

Gum

The gum can be replaced (the stamp is 'regummed'), or redistributed around an area where a hinge has been carefully removed. Or a stamp may be sweated (left in a sweat box to soften the gum) to remove a hinge and leave the stamp looking as though it is unmounted. When the gum on a stamp has been changed some of the glue works its way into the fibres of the paper. A tell-tale sign is that the stamp may curl the wrong way. The perforations are always much stiffer and their points feel sharp if lightly touched with a fingertip.

Perforations

Damaged perforations can be removed by carefully punching another row just inside the damaged section. This is quite common with stamps printed on thick paper and with widely spaced perforation holes, especially if the stamps have a high value. A typical example of this is the seahorse high values of Great Britain printed between 1913 and 1917. Watch out for stamps which are too small or with the perforations on one side not quite aligned properly.

Australia 1966–73, 15c stamp with rose-carmine missing which shows where the printing stopped and started.

Great Britain 1965 opening of the Post Office Tower, 3d stamp without tower.

Great Britain 1950-52 1d block, only partly perforated. This shows the point at which the perforating machine stopped working.

Postmarks

Sometimes these are also faked, particularly on older stamps where the catalogue value of a used example is greater than that of an unused one. Some recent issues have also had their postmarks faked, mainly where the price of a fine used set is greater than that of an unused one which has been heavily mounted.

ERRORS AND VARIETIES

All stamp collectors long to find a rare variety on their stamps. With new stamps printed in such large numbers it is not surprising that there are occasional misprints. Although the printers take great care to ensure that all the sheets with errors are destroyed, a few do pass through all the checking stages and are released to the Post Office without being noticed. The most valuable errors are stamps with missing colours or without perforations. Not only are these the most striking, but they are usually very scarce as only a few stamps on one sheet may be affected.

Other varieties are caused when the paper is folded before going into the perforating machine, or by a missing phosphor or other coating or a join in the paper where a new roll was started during the printing. Doctor blade flaws are caused when the blade (known as the doctor blade) which wipes the ink off the printing plate makes a mistake. This results in bands of colour running down the sheet. There are also numerous minor varieties which occur when the printing plate is made. These are called constant varieties because they are found in the same place in every sheet.

When any of the major varieties are found they create a lot of interest in the stamp world. The most valuable ones are those on a small part of one sheet, when a row of 5–10 stamps may be the only examples which exist. With so few available, it is not surprising that they sell for large sums!

Canada 1959 opening of the St Lawrence Seaway, 5c stamp with centre design upside down.

United States of America 1901 Pan-American Exposition, Buffalo 1c stamp with centre design printed upside down.

Great Britain 1962 National Productivity Year 1/3d with blue missing on upper stamp. The bottom stamp shows where the blue printing stopped.

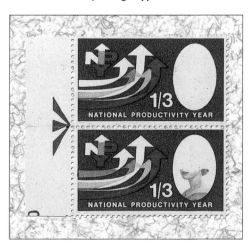

Stamps not Found in the Catalogue

The majority of stamps are produced and used for postage but they have also been used for many other purposes. Special non-postage stamps have been printed for specific purposes and they are just as interesting as the usual postage stamps, although they are not listed in stamp catalogues. Some collectors decide to specialize in these particular stamps.

This chapter is an introduction to the subject, intended as a helpful guide to recognizing any of these items that happen to find their way into your collection. There is also enough background information for anyone who wants to develop this area of collecting.

Revenue and fiscal stamps. Clockwise from top left: Great Britain land registry; United States proprietary stamp; United States match tax stamp; Hong Kong stamp duty; Great Britain transfer duty; Great Britain foreign bill; Hong Kong stamp duty.

REVENUE OR FISCAL STAMPS

One way in which the Government raised revenue at one time was to require a fee to be paid on all legal documents to make them valid. Special stamps were stuck on to the documents to show that the correct amount had been paid. Stamps were produced for each type of document including magistrates' and other courts, and for customs and medicine duty. The most usual use for revenue stamps was on receipts. All receipts had to have a penny stamp, which had to be signed in ink to be legal. The issue of the special receipt stamps was phased out in Great Britain in 1881, when the ordinary penny postage stamps were inscribed 'Postage and Revenue', to be used for both purposes. The receipt duty was at a later stage increased to twopence before being discontinued in the 1960s. You will probably see many stamps with a handwritten signature over them, or you may well discover the complete receipt. Some institutions which issued a large number of receipts overprinted their stamps with either the initials or the name of the company, both for the sake of convenience and to prevent their employees from stealing stamps.

TELEGRAPH STAMPS

These stamps are easily distinguished as they include the word 'Telegraph' (or something very similar) on their design. Even those stamps issued by Japan used a recognizable word. The cost of sending a telegram was paid in stamps which were then attached to a receipt. These were discontinued at the turn of the century when ordinary stamps could be used, so all telegraph stamps are quite old. Originally the telegraph service was run by private companies, each of which issued its own stamps. There are some interesting names, and some include the words 'Electric Telegraph' or 'Magnetic Telegraph' to emphasize the fact that the company used the latest technology.

Some telegraph offices also used special postmarks. For example, offices at racecourses had their own postmarks, such as Kempton Park Grandstand. This is a popular area of collecting.

A selection of Telegraph stamps.

RAILWAY STAMPS

The collecting of railway stamps is a large and sometimes specialized subject. As the railways did not interfere with the post office monopoly, letters, parcels and newspapers could be sent by train between railway stations and over to the Post Office for final delivery if the necessary postage stamps had been applied. It was an expensive method of sending letters and was only used when speed of delivery was important. However, parcels which were collected from the station were relatively cheap to send and a similar system is still in use today (Red Star), although the use of stamps ceased a long time ago.

Railway stamps were used mainly during the period before the major railway companies dominated the transport system, when there were many small lines each of which issued its own stamps. The different railway company names, and the nostalgia of the age of steam trains, adds to the popularity of these stamps.

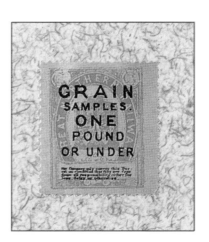

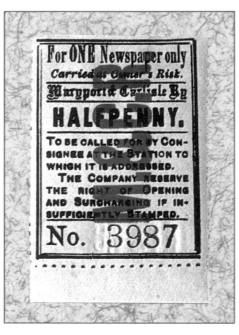

A selection of railway stamps.

A selection of local stamps.

LOCALS

These stamps were printed by letter delivery companies that operated independently from the Post Office, examples of which can be found from most countries. They were not valid for use outside the particular delivery company.

There were a number of such services in major towns around the world, particularly in China, Germany and Sweden. Here are a few examples:

★ **Australian Cycle Express, 1890s.** During the Australian gold rush cyclists carried mail from remote gold fields to the nearest main postal link, sometimes over a hundred miles away. By the mid-1890s camels were used as well as cyclists.

★ **Circular Delivery Company, 1865–7.** This provided local delivery of circulars at a much cheaper rate than the Post Office.

★ **College Stamps, 1871-94.** There was a delivery service around each college in Oxford and Cambridge.

★ **Court Bureau, 1890–1.** This was a Sunday collection from London clubs to the appropriate railway station to catch the mail train.

★ **Shipping Lines.** Various shipping lines provided postal services linking islands or connecting with mainland towns.

SAVINGS STAMPS

These were issued by the Post Office in order to encourage their customers to enter a savings scheme.

LABELS

These were often produced to commemorate an exhibition or other special philatelic event. Some of the early designs are colourful and elaborate. Other examples are labels produced for advertising purposes and other promotions. Some labels are still used. Unfortunately many are self-adhesive and do not hold the same attraction for stamp collectors.

A selection of attractive labels.

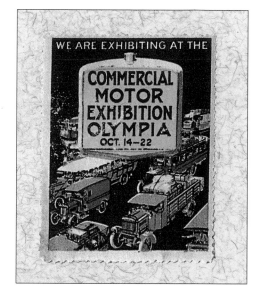

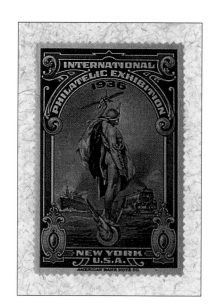

Philatelic Terms

Abnormal   An abnormal stamp is an example from a plate which was not officially issued, and is one of a few released in error. This term is usually only applied to British stamps. Most abnormals occurred during the issues of Queen Victoria.

Accountancy Mark   Before the establishment of the Universal Postal Union the amount charged by one country for delivering letters from another was agreed by special postal conventions. The amount due to the country of delivery was stamped on the cover and the totals were calculated periodically. These are sometimes called credit marks and are usually applied in red or black ink (see page 64).

Aerogramme   This is a flimsy letter sheet sold by the post office, already stamped for delivery anywhere in the world.

Airmail   This term is applied to a cover which has been carried on all or part of its journey by aeroplane. All covers should have the international airmail label. This also applies to stamps specially produced for airmail. The inscription will indicate this and the design usually features an aeroplane. Transport of letters by airmail was developed in the late 1920s and 1930s the period which most interests collectors.

Aniline   A water-soluble ink – usually a shade of red – which shows through to the back of the stamp.

Approvals   A term used for stamps which are sent out on a buy-or-return basis.

Auction   At auction stamps and collections are offered for sale to the highest bidder. A catalogue is produced listing all the lots for sale, which will often give an estimated value. There may be reserve price for some lots, meaning that they cannot be sold for less than that price.

Bisect   When they ran out of stamps of a certain value, the Post Office allowed a stamp of a higher value to be cut in half and both halves used in the normal way. Be wary of bisected stamps which are not listed in the catalogue – it is not uncommon for stamp collectors to cut stamps in half to see if they pass through the post – these are of no philatelic interest.

An abnormal 8d stamp printed in violet instead of orange-yellow.

A bisect stamp used on a cover sent from Singapore to Glasgow.

Block A block is where four or more stamps are still together in their original square or rectangular shape. It is often better to keep stamps in a block, especially if they are of an old issue. However, do not be worried about splitting blocks of modern stamps if one is required for your collection – there is no extra value in new blocks unless they show a special marking or variety.

Bogus Stamps These stamps do not represent any genuine country and were typically manufactured either as a joke or to deceive collectors.

Booklet For convenience stamps are often sold in small books. Stamps of different value are often printed side by side. (se-tenant). Earlier booklets with interleaving pages were either stitched or stapled at one side. Modern examples have the stamps fixed by their margin to one side of a folded card cover.

Booklet Pane A special sheet containing only a small number of stamps made for putting in a booklet.

Cachet This is a handstamped inscription applied to a cover giving details of a special event.

Catalogue A price list or guide. A stamp catalogue lists all the issued stamps with values for both unused and used examples. An auction catalogue describes lots for sale at that auction.

Charity Stamp Many countries produce stamps with an extra value printed on them. This additional revenue is donated to charity. The two countries which issue regular charity stamps are Switzerland (Pro Patria and Pro Juventute) and New Zealand (Health).

Cinderellas This term is reserved for those items which resemble postage stamps but are not official Government-issued postage stamps and are not listed in a standard catalogue. They include revenue stamps, local delivery stamps, telegraph stamps, railway stamps, savings stamps and various other labels. Specialist books and catalogues are available for many cinderellas.

Circular Date Stamp (c.d.s.) This is a circular postmark which shows the name of the town or city around the outside and has the date (sometimes the time as well) in the centre. Some of these postmarks have two circles around the outside – double-ring c.d.s.'s. These are the neatest postmarks and so are favoured by collectors.

Classic Classic stamps are the initial issue of stamps produced by those countries which first used postage stamps. The term is loosely used, but is usually applied to the majority of the first issues up to 1860, and to some of those issued up until 1875.

Coil Long coils of stamps were produced to fit into vending machines. The stamps may have been dispensed bottom first or sideways. With sideways-dispensed stamps, the watermark may appear sideways or the coil may have been made from ordinary sheets joined together, in which case there will be occasional joins in the strip. Some countries produce special coil stamps which are imperforate at the sides of the coil.

Coil Leader This is a strip of paper at the beginning of the coil. It is printed with details of the stamps, the values and the number of stamps in the coil. These are used to thread the coil through the vending machine. There is a shorter strip of paper at the end of the coil and this is called the **coil follower.**

Colour Changeling This term is used for a stamp which has had its colour changed by being soaked in water or by long exposure to sunlight. This is most dramatic with some green colours, which can turn to a delicate shade of blue.

Colour Trial In recess and typograph printing the design is prepared first. Once the engraved die has been approved the correct colours need to be chosen. Usually one of the dies is printed in a range of colours which are sent off for approval.

Commercial Cover These are usually commercial letters. Ordinary correspondence can also be classified as commercial to distinguish it from philatelic covers.

Thematic collecting: flowers on stamps (page 60), recently used as a way of publicising the possible extinction of endangered species.

A block of 10 stamps (Great Britain King George VI 6d) showing a striking example of the doctor blade flaw.

Cover A cover applies to the outer covering of any item sent by post. This may be an envelope or a wrapper. Envelopes are now standard but in those days when letters were first sent by post, envelopes were relatively expensive and not often used. The usual practice then was to fold another sheet of paper around the outside of the letter and fasten it with sealing wax.

Cylinder Number Each printing cylinder is given a number and this is printed in the margin of the sheet of stamps. In multi-coloured printing the cylinder numbers are printed in a row. If one of the colour cylinders becomes defective a new one is prepared with the next number. Sometimes there is a gap in the numbering because the replacement printing cylinder was found unsuitable and destroyed.

Dandy Roll This is a drum used in the production of paper. If a watermark is required in the paper the 'bits' are stuck on to the dandy roll (see page 40).

Die The designs of recess printed and typographed stamps are initially engraved on to a steel plate which is called the die (see page 44).

Die Proof This is a printed impression taken from the die to check for any small defects in the engraving or to be sent to the postal authorities for their approval. Die proofs are printed on either thin wove paper or glazed card, depending on the printers.

Doctor Blade This blade runs over the printing cylinder to remove the unwanted ink. If the printing stops at all then parallel lines of ink are left each side of the spot where the doctor blade was touching the cylinder. These two lines of colour are called doctor blade flaws and can be quite spectacular if the printing stopped for any length of time.

Dry Print If the ink in one of the printing cylinders runs very low, less ink is transferred to the printing plate. Where this happens the depth of colour is reduced and the result is called a dry print.

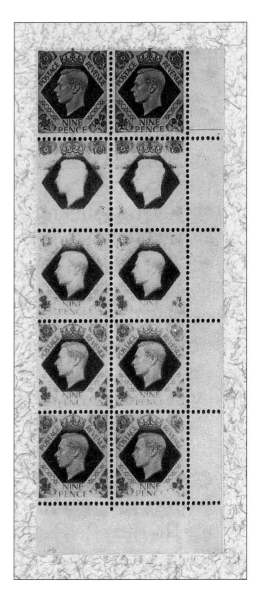

A corner block of 10 stamps (Great Britain King George VI 9d) showing a dramatic dry print variety.

SOUVENIR PACKETS

Post offices around the world issue souvenir packets celebrating exhibitions, festivals, centenaries, national heroes and important sporting occasions! Older examples are becoming increasingly collectible. The two featured here highlight elements of Australia's history and wildlife.

Entire or Entire Letter   This term applies to early mail where an outer wrapper was used instead of a letter (see **cover**). The letter often contains useful information which may not be given on the outside, such as the date and place of writing. These covers are thus distinguished from those where only the outer wrapper has survived.

Essay   This is the artwork for a proposed stamp design. Usually it is the painted design which is submitted. Sometimes the artwork progresses further and the essay may be in the form of a photographic reduction to stamp size.

Fancy Cancel   This term is applied to some illustrated postmarks used in the United States between 1850 and 1900. Many postmasters made their own cancellers from wood or cork, and some of their designs were quite decorative, including bees, eagles, pigs, hearts, masonic symbols, flags and heads.

First-Day Cover   This is a cover bearing a stamp (or set of stamps) posted on the day of issue. First-day cover collecting has become popular and the post office issues special covers for each new issue. These covers have an illustration depicting an aspect of the subject of the issue and often include a card which gives further details of the subject.

First-Flight Cover   When air transport was in its infancy in the early 1930s many new routes were being established. As with first-day covers, it was soon fashionable to collect covers which were carried on the first mail-carrying flights between different towns or countries.

Fly Specks   Small varieties on the designs of stamps. These minor errors are created when the designs are laid out on the printing cylinder and are repeated in the same position on each sheet. Be wary of collecting varieties which can only be seen with a powerful magnifying glass – they soon make a boring collection!

Forwarding Agents   In the early days of the postal service, sending international letters could be very expensive. To save money it was possible to arrange to have mail sent by forwarding agents. They would carry letters privately to the country of destination to be posted. These letters had the handstamp of the forwarding agents applied to either the front or the back of the cover.

Frank   This is an alternative name for a postmark.

Gutter Margins   Sometimes sheets of stamps are issued in one or more panes. The margin between these panes is called the gutter margin. Sometimes it is called the interpanneau margin, although this term is usually restricted to older stamps.

Imperforate   A stamp issued without any perforations is said to be imperforate. Many of the first stamps issued were imperforate and had to be cut from the sheet with scissors. Some modern stamps are found without perforations when the perforating machine has malfunctioned, and these can be worth a lot of money.

This pair of Christmas stamps shows a gutter margin which runs down the middle of a sheet of stamps. The printer's 'traffic lights' are shown on the gutter margin.

Three stamps from Straights Settlements showing similar designs used during the reigns of three monarchs. The same basic design for each of the monarchs was used for many of the British colonies.

Imprimatur This is a term applied to British Victorian stamps which have been cut from imperforate sheets stored at the post office. One sheet of each value and different plate number was kept for archive and reference purposes. A few examples from these sheets were removed to be given to certain officials.

India Paper This is a very thin paper sometimes used for die proofs. Once printed it is stuck to card to prevent it tearing.

Instructional Marks These are hand-struck marks applied to envelopes giving instructions or comments, such as 'Found Without Contents', 'Posted Without Address', 'Return To Sender'.

Joins Coils of stamps are sometimes made up of stamps printed in normal sheets which are then joined together and divided into single rows. The sheets are joined by leaving a narrow margin on one side to which the next sheet is stuck. This junction is called a **coil join.** When the roll of paper running through the printing press runs out the next roll is stuck to the end so that the printing process remains continuous. This is called a **paper join.** Occasionally the paper tears in the printing press and has to be repaired. These are more interesting if the repair is made before the stamps are perforated.

Key Plate Between the 1890s and 1930s some of the colonial powers such as Great Britain and Portugal used the same design of stamp for several different colonies. These basic designs are called key types or key plates.

Kiloware Stamps on paper sold by weight are called kiloware. Look out for different categories such as stamps of your own country, either definitives or commemoratives, and foreign stamps.

Maximum Card This is a postcard which features the design of the stamp or an enlarged picture of it. In Britain these are now called PHQ cards after the coding number given to them by the Post Office.

Meter Mail Special machines can be rented from the post office which print the cost of postage on a label or directly on to the envelope. The amount of postage used is then paid periodically. The term is derived from the meters built into these machines which register the amount of postage paid.

Miniature Sheet Sometimes one value or a set is printed in a special mini-sheet, or sheetlet, for collectors.

A miniature sheet showing one stamp as part of the overall design.

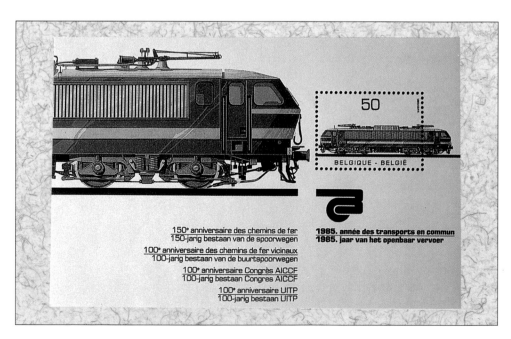

Mint   Technically a mint stamp is in the same condition as when it was sold at the post office. However, the term is often applied to any unused stamps. Many dealers use mint to describe unused stamps in a range of conditions: unmounted; lightly mounted (stamps with a faint trace of a peeled-off hinge); large part original gum (o.g. means that although there is much of the original gum left, the stamp has had several hinges, or one large hinge, removed); and without gum.

Multipositive   One of the printing plates used in the photogravure printing method.

Officials   Government departments used stamps specially printed or regular stamps overprinted with the relevant department. This system was not particularly efficient and today prepaid envelopes are used instead. In Britian these include the letters OHMS (On Her Majesty's Service).

Off-set   If the printing ink is still damp when the sheets are stacked, part or all of the design appears on the gum of the top sheet. This is known as off-set. This variety is occasionally to be found on stamps printed typographically because the sheets are printed one at a time, so it is possible for the next sheet to be printed and stacked quite quickly.

Omnibus   When a special event is celebrated on the stamps of many different countries the collective term for these are omnibus issues. Those countries which have their issues controlled by the Crown Agents issue stamps with similar designs.

Overprint   This is a surcharge or text printed on to a stamp.

Paquebot   A letter posted at sea will use the stamps from the last port of call or the country of origin. These letters are accepted in a foreign country and cancelled with a paquebot cancel in either a straight line or circular date stamp.

Perfin   At one time some companies had their initials perforated into their stamps to prevent unauthorized use by employees. These are most easily seen from the back of the stamp. Although a few people do collect perfins, they usually make the stamp valueless.

Perforations   These are the holes punched around stamps to ease their removal from the sheet (see page 41).

Philatelic Covers   Many covers are posted by collectors, and these types of covers are called philatelic. It is far better to have a cover which has not been specially posted.

Philately   More than just stamp collecting, this is the study of all things related to mail and postal services.

Philatelist   This term is used for a stamp collector, but to be correct it should only be used for someone who studies stamps and aspects of their use.

Phosphor Band   To activate automatic letter-facing machines a phosphorescent material was printed in bands on the stamps. Phosphor bands can be seen by holding the stamp at an angle to the light. They have now been replaced by additives in either the paper or special coatings (see page 45).

Plate   This refers to the printing plate used in the recess and typographic printing methods. Each printing plate is coded with its own plate number.

Plate Proof   This is an imperforate trial sheet taken from a new plate to be examined in minute detail to check for any flaws which need to be corrected.

Postage Due   This term refers to the stamps used on underpaid letters. For details of how these charges are calculated see page 68.

Postal History   This is the term used for covers which give information or tell a story about some area of the postal service.

Postal Stationery   Postal stationery consists of pre-stamped envelopes and cards sold by the Post Office (see page 13).

Precancel   Stamps which have a cancellation applied before being used for postage are precancelled. It usually only applies to American stamps, which show the name of the post office between horizontal lines.

A stamp viewed from the back to show the perfin 'C O X'.

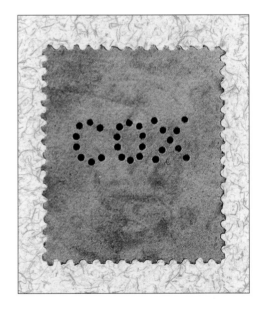

They were used by companies in order to reduce handling and speed up the mail.

Presentation Pack Sold by the Post Office, these contain a set of stamps plus additional interesting information.

Pre-Stamp Cover This is a letter sent before the introduction of adhesive postage stamps. The amount due was usually written on the face of the cover in ink.

Proof This is an impression of a stamp made by the printers during the preparation of the printing plates. Different proofs may be produced at different stages of production, like die proofs, plate proofs, or colour trials. They are nearly always without perforations.

Provisionals These are stamps produced locally to overcome a shortage of certain national values before regular supplies are re-established. The usual practice was to overprint or surcharge stamps which were still in plentiful supply. Occasionally a new design was made and printed – these were usually fairly crude affairs.

Rate Mark Before postage stamps were used, the cost of sending a letter was either written or handstamped on the front of the letter. Although both of these are rate marks, the term is more correctly used for those charges applied by a handstamp.

Remainders An occasional practice during the last century was for postal authorities to sell off surplus stocks of stamps. If they were no longer valid for use on letters they were sold to dealers at discounted prices. When stamps have been remaindered the catalogue value for unused examples is usually much less than that of used stamps.

Reprint Later printings of postage stamps were sometimes produced especially to satisfy the demands by collectors for examples of the early issues. These are called reprints (see page 74).

Se-tenant This term refers to stamps of different values printed side by side. Se-tenant stamps are usually found in booklets or on miniature sheets.

Slogan Postmark This is a machine postmark with a circular datestamp to one side of an advertisement or announcement.

Space-Filler This term refers to a damaged stamp mounted in a collection until such a time when a better example can be found to replace it.

Specimen A stamp is overprinted SPECIMEN when it is sent out for promotional or similar purpose. Most specimen stamps occurred between the 1870s and 1940s when the Universal Postal Union needed enough examples of every new stamp to send to all the participating nations so that they would know which stamps were valid from the different countries. Nowadays, countries do not bother to overprint their stamps and the only specimens are manufactured by a small number of countries as part of their press releases or for give-away promotions.

Surcharge When a new value is overprinted on an existing stamp, it is said to be surcharged. Surcharges are usually made because supplies of a particular value have run low or a new postage rate is introduced before suitable values become available.

Sweat Box This is a sealed container with a damp sponge or something similar. It creates a humid atmosphere to soften the gum of unused stamps so that old hinges can be removed without leaving a mark. The results of using a sweat box are mixed and an expert can easily tell when a stamp has been 'sweated'.

Tax Mark This is a handstamp indicating that a letter is underpaid. Some tax marks also show the amount which is due.

Tête-bêche This term refers to two stamps printed together but with one design printed upside down. They come from sheets printed for booklets.

Tied A stamp is said to be tied to a cover when the postmark covers both the stamp and the cover. This proves that the stamp belongs to the cover.

Traffic Lights Sheets of stamps usually show the cylinder numbers at one side with

Opposite top:
A strip of five stamps taken from a coil, showing different values se-tenant.

Opposite left:
An overprint 'SPECIMEN' on a pair of imperforate King George V ld stamps.

Opposite right:
A Jordanian stamp showing a local surcharge over an existing overprint.

Opposite middle:
Two South African halfpenny stamps, showing a tête-bêche.

Opposite bottom:
A corner block of six stamps showing traffic light colours at the top. Note that the block also shows a paper fold in the top right corner causing the perforations to be made at an incorrect angle.

coloured circles on the other. You may wonder how on earth this name originated with the multicoloured printing which is common today, but the name was first used when commemorative stamps were printed in three colours, vaguely resembling traffic lights.

Transit Marks These are postmarks applied to a cover between posting and delivery. It was usual for all mail to be postmarked each time it was sorted and international letters might receive two or three transit marks.

Underprint This is text printed on the back of a stamp. In Britain underprints were used before the introduction of perfins. In these cases the name of the company was printed on the paper before it was gummed. Later British examples of underprints were printed on top of the gum. In 1893 stamps of New Zealand were issued with a variety of commercial advertisements on the back. They were printed before the stamps were gummed and can be collected in used condition. Advertisements for Pear's Soap, used as experiments in the 1890s are also available.

Unmounted Mint This refers to an unused stamp which has not been mounted with a stamp hinge, so that the gum is in perfect condition.

Used Abroad When a stamp from one country has been used in one of its postal agencies in a foreign country, it is said to have been used abroad (see page 69).

Vignette These labels applied to covers typically advertise an event associated with the cover, or give special instructions.

Watermark This is an impressed pattern made in the paper during its manufacture. The watermark can be seen as a slight thinning of the paper in a regular pattern.

Wrapper This is a sheet of paper folded around a letter and fastened with wax or a special seal. Wrappers were used before envelopes were cheap enough for general use.

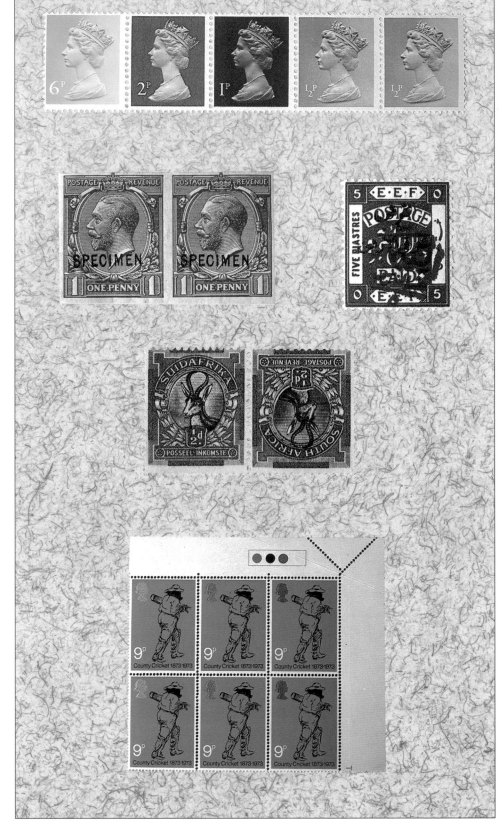

Index

Note. Captions to illustrations are indicated by *italic* page numbers.

PICTURE CREDITS

Trevor Wood: pages 9, 11 (top), 12 (top), 13 (bottom), 17–21, 23–28 (bottom), 31, 34, 36–40, 42 (bottom left), 43 (bottom), 45, 47, 50–55, 57–63, 64 (bottom), 65–71, 73, 74 (right), 75, 76 (left), 77 (top), 79–83, 86, 87 (left), 88–92, 93 (below top/below middle)

Stanley Gibbons Ltd: pages 11 (top), 12 (bottom), 13 (top), 14, 15, 28 (top), 42 (top/bottom right), 43 (top), 44, 64 (top/middle), 74 (left), 76 (right), 77 (bottom), 85, 87 (right), 93 (top/middle)

All stamps, equipment etc. photographed in this book were supplied by Stanley Gibbons Ltd.